D1416177

3574500023624

THE GREAT
FABRIC DOLL
BOOK

THE GREAT
FABRIC DOLL
BOOK

A Family Workshop Book
By Ed and Stevie Baldwin

DOUBLEDAY & COMPANY, INC.
GARDEN CITY, NEW YORK
1986

Created by The Family Workshop, Inc.
Executive Editor: Janet Weberling
Editors: Suzi West, Robert Hill
Art Director: Wanda Young
Production Artists: Janice Harris Burstall, Roberta Taff
Typography: Kathy Dolbow
Project Designs: Stevie Baldwin, April Bail
Photography: Bill Welch
Traffic Coordinator: S.P. Bob

The information in this book is correct and complete to the best of our knowledge. All recommendations are made without guarantees on the part of the authors or Doubleday & Company, Inc., who disclaim all liability in connection with the use of this information.

The Family Workshop's catalog of project plans is available for $2.95 from: The Family Workshop, Inc., P.O. Box 1000, Bixby OK 74008

Library of Congress Cataloging-in-Publication Data
Main entry under title:

The Great fabric doll book.

   1. Dollmaking.   2. Soft toy making.   3. Family Workshop, Inc.
TT175.G719 1986   745.592'21   85-16292
ISBN: 0-385-23574-7 (hc)
ISBN: 0-385-19711-X (pbk)

Library of Congress Catalog Card Number 85-16292
Copyright © 1986 by The Family Workshop, Inc.
All Rights Reserved
Printed in the United States of America
First Edition

To Sean, Holly and Rachel Bail,
the best friends a mother could ever have.

Contents

Tips & Techniques

Whether you are a wizard or a greenhorn at making fabric dolls, you may wish to scan this section before beginning work on the projects. In addition to basic sewing definitions and instructions for enlarging scale drawings, it includes brief discussions of embroidery, buttonholes, zippers, applique, fabric painting, working with nylon hose and soft-sculpting.

ENLARGING SCALE DRAWINGS

A scale drawing appears on a background grid of small squares and includes a legend at the top that specifies the scale: 1 square = 1 inch. There are several ways to enlarge the drawing to full size:

Pantograph: A pantograph is a tool containing several joined rods and two styli (pencil leads). As you trace the scale drawing, using the guide stylus, the secondary stylus draws the full-size pattern simultaneously.

Opaque Projector: Place the scale drawing in the projector and aim it at a flat wall. Move the unit forward or backward until the projected squares of the grid measure exactly 1 inch square. Tape paper to the wall and trace the outlines of the patterns.

Grid Paper: For this method you'll need paper containing a grid of 1-inch squares (drafting paper or dressmaker's pattern paper). To make the full-size pattern (**Figure A**), work one square at a time as you reproduce onto the full-size grid the lines that appear on the scale drawing.

SEWING & FABRIC TIPS

The Basics

Fabric: We specify the types and colors of fabric that we used for each project. Feel free to substitute, but choose similar weights and finishes. Launder and press the fabrics to prevent shrinkage problems later.

Patterns: When you are instructed to cut two (or more) fabric pieces from one pattern, double the fabric and cut both at once, so the resulting pieces will be mirror images of each other. Transfer to the fabric pieces all placement markings that appear on the pattern.

Half-Patterns: Most symmetrical patterns are provided as half-patterns and the words "Place on Fold" appear along one edge. Double the fabric and place the designated edge of the pattern along the fold line. Do not cut along the fold.

Seam Allowance: On all patterns a solid line indicates the outer edge (cutting line) and a broken line indicates the seam line. The area between the two is the seam allowance.

Clipping Curves and Corners: Some seam allowances must be clipped so the fabric will lie flat when it is turned right side out. Take care not to cut the seam. Clip curves, as shown in **Figure B**. Clip corners by cutting off the corner of the allowance.

Circular Patterns: To draw a large circle, place your tape measure on the fabric and insert a pin through it and into the fabric where the center of the circle will be. Measure from the pin a distance equal to the radius of the circle and make a small

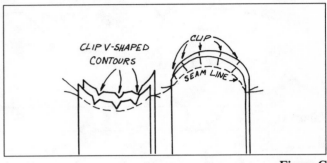

CLIP V-SHAPED CONTOURS
CLIP
SEAM LINE

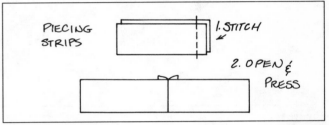

Figure C

PIECING STRIPS
1. STITCH
2. OPEN & PRESS

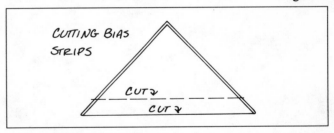

CUTTING BIAS STRIPS
CUT
CUT

hole in the tape. Insert the tip of a pen through the hole and draw the circle as you rotate the pen and tape measure around the pinned center point.

Piecing Strips: To make a long fabric strip, you may have to piece together several shorter ones. Place two strips right sides together and stitch the seam (**Figure C**). Press the seam open. Continue adding strips in this manner until the desired length is achieved.

Bias Strips: Use bias strips to bind curved edges and to make piping, because they are stretchy and will not wrinkle. To cut bias strips, first cut a fabric square along the grain. Fold the square in half diagonally and cut through both layers (**Figure D**) to the desired width.

Figure E

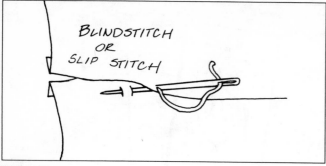

Figure F

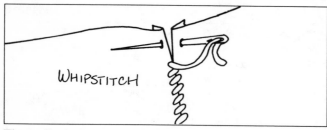

Figure G

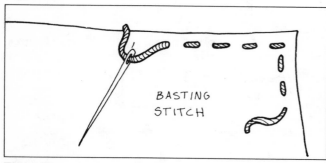

Figure H

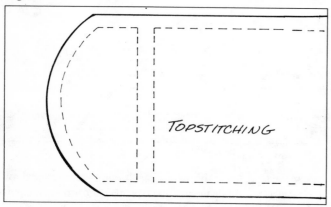

Blindstitch or Slip Stitch: This hand stitch produces an almost invisible seam (**Figure E**). Slide the needle through the top fabric, then pick up a small stitch on the bottom fabric. Keep the stitches evenly spaced.

Whipstitch: Use the whipstitch when fast-and-easy is more important than neatness, because it will show (**Figure F**).

Basting: Basting stitches are used to secure an assembly temporarily and also in gathering. To hand baste (**Figure G**), make running stitches about ½ inch long. To machine baste, set your stitch selector to the longest straight stitch. Use a contrasting thread color that is easy to see.

Topstitch: This is a final stitch on the right side of the fabric. It should be as straight as possible and a uniform distance from the edge or seam (**Figure H**).

Glueing: Glue can often be used in place of stitches. If you use white glue, pin or clothespin the assembly while the glue dries. We prefer hot-melt adhesive, which is used with a glue gun. It sets up very fast and forms a strong waterproof bond. Use hot glue carefully, as it will blister your fingers if touched too soon.

Embroidery

Cotton embroidery floss is composed of six twisted strands, which can be separated. The fewer strands you use, the finer the finished work will look. Use an embroidery hoop to hold the fabric flat. Several embroidery stitches used in this book are illustrated in **Figure I**.

Counted cross-stitch looks best on an even-weave fabric such as linen or aida cloth. Two rows of cross-stitches are shown in **Figure J**. The blunt-tipped tapestry needle is inserted through the holes between the fabric threads. Each cross-stitch consists of two straight stitches, one crossed over the other. Be sure to cross each stitch in the same direction, as indicated by the "right" and "wrong" diagrams. To follow a cross-stitch graph, start in the center so your design will be centered on the fabric. Legs of adjacent stitches should share the same holes, unless a space is indicated on the graph. Count the stitches shown on the graph and work the same number of cross-stitches on the fabric.

Buttonholes

Buttonholes can be worked by hand or machine, but the latter is fastest and easiest. You'll need a machine with a buttonhole attachment or zigzag capabilities; otherwise, bind the edges of the buttonhole by working closely spaced hand blanket stitches.

Placement of the buttonhole should be marked on the fabric. The length should be ¼ inch longer than the diameter of the button, to allow for the bartack at each end (see **Figure K**). If your machine has a buttonhole attachment, follow the instructions provided with it. If not, follow the steps listed here.

1. Set stitch selectors for closely spaced, medium-width zigzag. Work one edge of buttonhole (**Figure K**, step a).

2. Rotate fabric 180 degrees and take one stitch to move needle to left (step b, **Figure K**).

3. Reset stitch selector to widest zigzag and stitch bartack (step c), ⅛ inch long.

4. Reset to medium zigzag and stitch second edge of buttonhole (step d), stopping ⅛ inch from end.

5. Reset to widest zigzag and stitch bartack (step e).

6. Use small sharp scissors or blade to cut open (step e). Don't cut through bartack stitches.

Zippers

When working with delicate or stretchy fabrics or those with thick pile, it's best to hand stitch the zipper in place. Use a tiny

Figure I

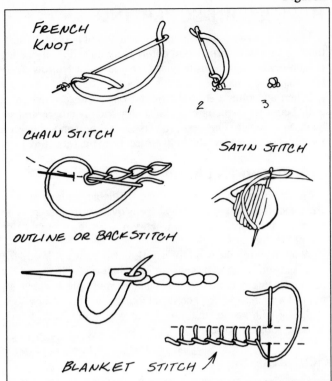

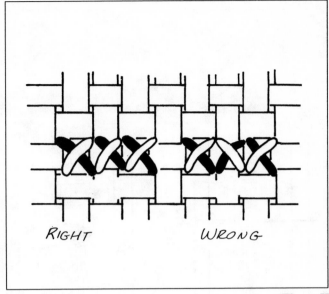

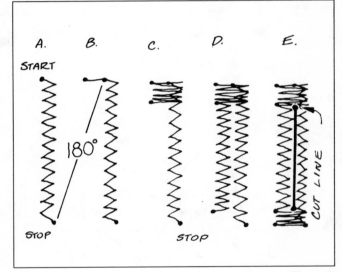

Figure L

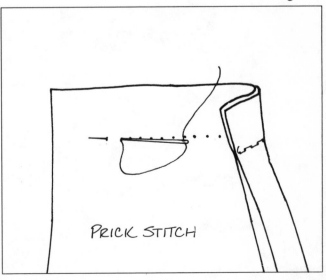

prick stitch (**Figure L**). To shorten a zipper, first baste it into the zipper opening. Whipstitch across the zipper teeth ¼ inch below the end of the fabric opening (**Figure M**). Sew a metal eye-bar above the whipstitches, as shown. Cut off the excess zipper ½ inch below.

Applique

An applique is a decorative fabric piece that is attached to a larger background piece or garment. Here are a couple of methods of attaching appliques:

Method 1: Cut applique with a ⅜-inch seam allowance. Pin or baste to the larger fabric, placing fiberfill underneath for a puffy look. Run closely spaced machine zigzag stitches around seam line (**Figure N**). Trim seam allowance close to stitches, being careful not to cut stitches.

Method 2: Cut applique with no seam allowance. Zigzag around edge, making sure the needle penetrates both applique and background fabric.

Method 3: Cut applique with a ¼-inch seam allowance, and press allowance to wrong side. Hand stitch, using closely spaced blanket stitch.

Method 4: Cut applique with no seam allowance. Adhere to larger fabric using glue or fusible interfacing. Stitch around edge by hand or machine.

Fabric Painting

Acrylic paint straight from the tube is a good thickness for most fabrics. Thin paint will bleed into the fabric; thick paint will not penetrate. Test on a piece of scrap fabric. Acrylic paints are water-soluble, but once dry, they are permanent.

Figure M

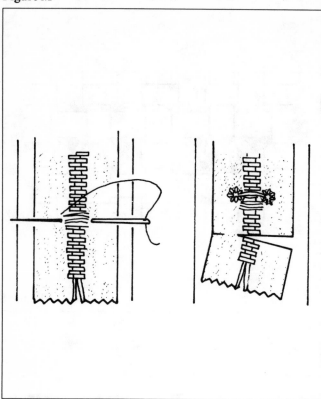

Figure N

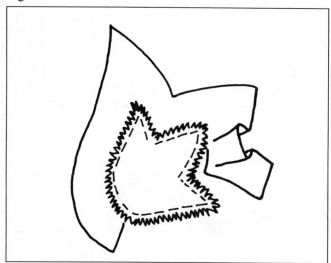

HOSE & SOFT-SCULPTING

Unless otherwise specified, use normal-weight hose. "Flesh-tone" means any normal skin color. Only a portion of one leg is required to make a stuffed head, so you can use throw-away hose that have runs.

When attaching a stuffed pantyhose head to the body of a doll, begin whipstitching at the center back – otherwise, the head will swivel. Finished projects should be sprayed with a light coat of clear acrylic to help protect from runs and dirt.

Stuffing and Shaping

Stuffed hose are very pliable and moldable, as long as they are not stuffed too tightly. If a shape is over-stuffed, there is no room for the fiberfill to give when you wish to manipulate or sculpt a feature.

When forming the head for a doll, insert your fist inside the hose and stuff around it, so there is a small cavity in the center of the stuffing. Manipulate the shape to resemble a real head, not just a round sphere. The facial features are created by soft-sculpting with needle and thread, but you want to start with a realistic-looking shape.

Sculpting

A type of needle called a "sharp" is best for sculpting. Use a long one, so it won't get lost inside large stuffed forms. The best sculpting thread is heavy-duty 100% nylon with a bonded finish, normally used for drapery making.

An 18-inch strand of thread is sufficient to sculpt the facial features on most dolls. Diagrams provided with the instructions show the points at which you enter and exit the needle. Mark the points on the head before you start sculpting.

When the instructions read "reenter at the same point," insert the needle as close as possible to the last exit point. When you pull the thread to define a sculpted area, be careful not to rip the hose. To secure the defined area, take a couple of small stitches at the exit point; this is called "lock the stitch."

If you see a run begin to develop, apply clear fingernail polish. If you run out of thread, lock the stitch and cut the thread. Rethread your needle, reenter at point 1, exit where you locked off and continue sculpting from there. The most important thing to remember is that you don't have to settle for what you get the first time. You can remove sculpting stitches and you can even turn a head around and use the back if you don't like what you did on the front.

Victoria

Meet Victoria, the reigning queen of the doll world. She stands a regal 21 inches tall and wears ultra-luxurious clothing in velvet and taffeta, eyelet and lace. She wears soft leather high-top boots and would never be seen in public without her white lace gloves. From the tip of her slightly snooty nose to her oh-so-proper bloomers, Victoria (never Vicki) is the epitome of social grace and charm.

Materials

One leg of regular-weave flesh-tone hose
½ yard of blue velvet
¼ yard of beige soft leather or textured vinyl
½ yard of white eyelet fabric
8-inch square of lace fabric
½ yard of white taffeta
½ yard of flesh-tone cotton knit
½ yard of 5-inch white eyelet trim
12-inch length of 1½-inch gold, bead and lace trim
6-inch length of 2-inch ornate trim (We used white pleated satin with lace on each side.)
½ yard of 1- or ¾-inch white satin ribbon
One package of ¼-inch elastic
Small section of blonde wiglet for the hair
Half pound of polyester fiberfill
One hook-and-eye closure
Earrings; cosmetic cheek blusher; and blonde hairpins
Long sharp needle; heavy-duty thread in white and flesh-tone; and regular thread in blue, white and flesh-tone
Hot-melt glue and a glue gun (or white glue)
Acrylic paints in red, white and black; and a fine-tipped artist's brush

Cutting the Pieces

1. A full-size pattern for the Boot is provided in **Figure A**. Trace the pattern onto tracing paper or dressmaker's paper.

2. Scale drawings are provided for the Blouse Back, Blouse Front, Torso, Bloomers, Sleeve and Arm in **Figure B**. Enlarge the drawings to make full-size paper patterns. (Refer to Tips & Techniques, if necessary.)

3. Cut the pieces as listed in this step from the specified types and colors of fabric.

Blue velvet:
    Skirt – cut one, 12 x 32 inches
Flesh-tone cotton knit:
    Arm – cut four
    Leg – cut four, 3⅛ x 5½ inches
    Torso – cut two
Beige leather or vinyl:
    Boot – cut four
White lace fabric:
    Glove – cut four
White eyelet fabric:
    Blouse Front – cut one
    Blouse Back – cut two
    Sleeve – cut two
White taffeta:
    Slip – cut one, 12 x 16 inches
    Sash – cut one, 6 x 30 inches
    Bloomers – cut two

Making the Body

Note: All seams are ⅜ inch unless otherwise specified.

1. Place two Arms right sides together and stitch the contoured seam, leaving the shoulder open (**Figure C**). Clip the curves, turn right side out and press. Lightly stuff the arm with fiberfill, leaving ½ inch unstuffed at the shoulder edge.

2. Make another arm in the same manner, using the two remaining Arm pieces.

Figure A

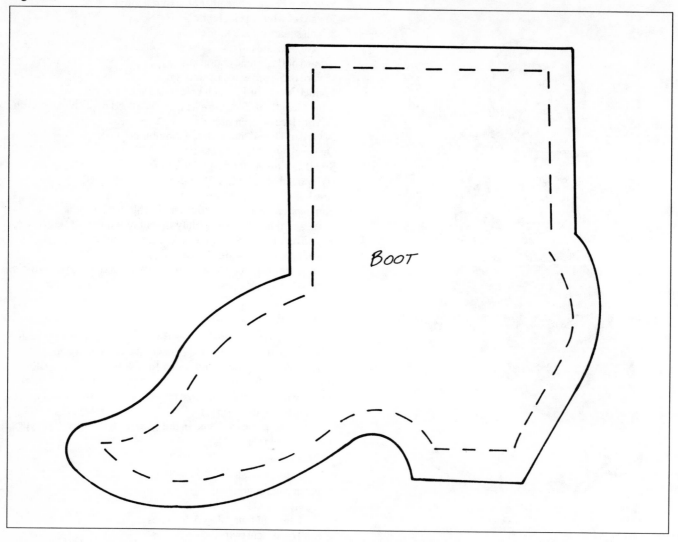

BOOT

3. Place the short edge of one Leg and the top edge of one Boot right sides together. Stitch the seam, as shown in **Figure D**, and press open. Repeat this step three more times, using the remaining Boot and Leg pieces.

4. Place two of the leg-and-boot assemblies right sides together (**Figure E**) and stitch along the seam line, leaving the straight top edge open. Repeat this step, using the remaining two leg-and-boot assemblies. Clip the corners and curves and turn each leg right side out. Stuff the boots tightly. Stuff and manipulate the legs, leaving the top ½ inch unstuffed.

5. Place the two Torsos right sides together. Stitch the seams, leaving the neck and lower edges open, as shown in **Figure F**. Clip the corners and turn the torso right side out.

6. Pin the tops of the legs to the lower edge of the front torso, with the toes pointing toward the body (**Figure G**). Stitch ¼ inch from the edge, attaching the legs to the front torso only.

7. Stuff the torso, leaving ½ inch unstuffed at the bottom and at the neck.

8. Turn the legs downward and turn a ¼-inch seam allowance to the inside around the remaining portion of the lower edge. Whipstitch the folded edges together.

9. Whipstitch the arms to the torso, making sure they are turned with the thumbs pointing upward (**Figure H**).

10. Place two Gloves right sides together and sew a ¼-inch seam around the outer edge, leaving the wrist open. Clip the corners and curves. Turn the glove right side out. Turn under and stitch a tiny hem around the wrist. Fit the finished glove over Victoria's hand. Make a second glove in the same manner, using the remaining two Glove pieces.

11. To soft-sculpt the fingers over the gloves (which is the reason Victoria is never seen in public without her gloves), use a long sharp needle and white heavy-duty thread. Follow the entry and exit points illustrated in **Figure I**.

    a. Enter at point 1 on the palm of the hand and exit directly opposite point 1 on the back of the hand. This will be the base of the first finger.

    b. Wrap the thread around the end of the hand, reenter at 1 on the palm and exit at 1 on the back. Pull the thread tightly to form the first finger and lock the stitch at 1.

    c. Reenter at 1, push the needle underneath the surface and exit at 2 on the back of the hand. This is the base of the second finger.

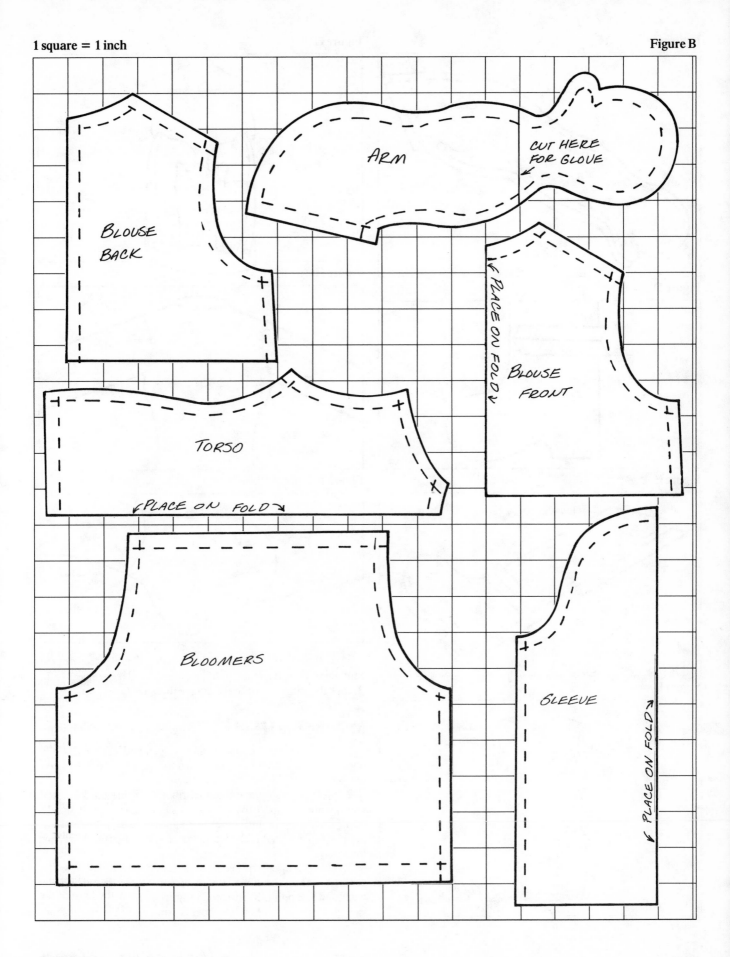

Arm

CUT HERE
FOR GLOVE

BLOUSE
BACK

PLACE ON FOLD

BLOUSE
FRONT

TORSO

←PLACE ON FOLD→

BLOOMERS

SLEEVE

←PLACE ON FOLD→

Figure C

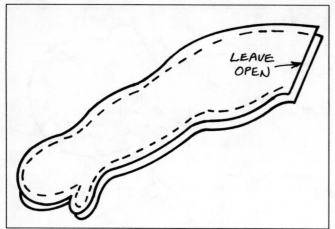

Figure D

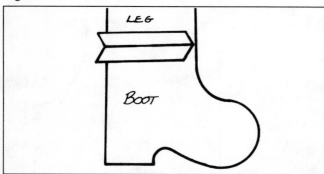

Figure E

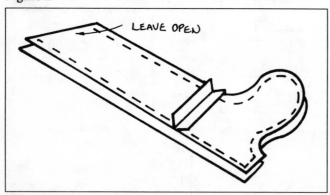

Figure F

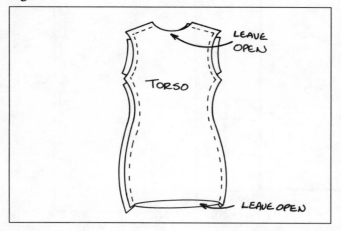

Figure G

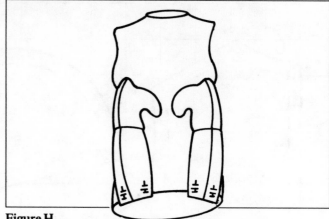

Figure H

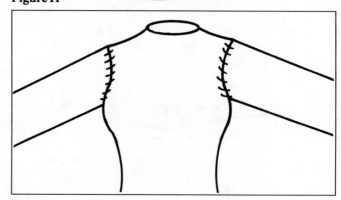

Figure I

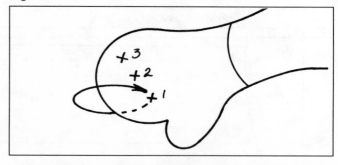

d. Repeat sub-steps b and c at points 2 and 3 to form the remaining fingers. When you have completed the steps at point 3, lock the stitch securely and cut the thread.

Making the Head

1. Tie a knot in the hose near the open end. Cut across the hose 6 inches below the knot. Turn the hose so the knot is on the inside.

2. Stuff a generous amount of fiberfill inside the hose and manipulate the fiberfill until a head shape is formed. It should be 12 inches in circumference and approximately 4½ inches in diameter. Tie a knot in the stuffed hose at the open end to secure the fiberfill.

3. Use a long sharp needle and heavy-duty thread to soft-sculpt the facial features. Begin with the nose, following the entry and exit points illustrated in **Figure J**.

a. Enter at 1 where the hose is knotted at the neck. Push

Victoria
page 13

Muffy
page 21

Kim Sue, Muffy & Fredd Redd
page 21

Zippity-Do-Tie
page 44

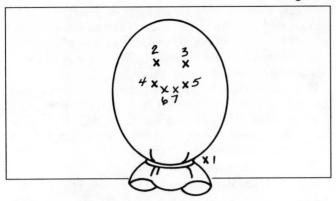

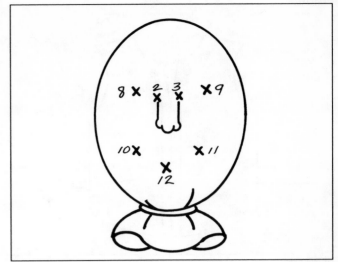

Figure L

the needle through the head and exit at 2.

   b. To form the nose, pull the thread across the surface, enter at 4 and exit at 3. Pull the thread across the surface, enter at 5 and exit at 2. Gently pull the thread until the straight bridge of the nose forms. Lock the stitch at point 2.

   c. To form the nostrils, reenter at 2 and exit at 6. Enter ¼ inch above 6 and exit at 3. Pull the thread until the nostril forms and lock the stitch at 3.

   d. Reenter at 3 and exit at 7. Enter ¼ inch above 7 and exit at 2. Pull the thread until the second nostril forms and lock the stitch at 2. Do not cut the thread.

4. Victoria's eye lines and mouth line are soft-sculpted. Her open eyes and lips are later painted. Continue with the same thread to sculpt the eyes and mouth. Follow the entry and exit points illustrated in **Figure K**.

   a. Pull the thread across the surface, enter at 8 and exit at point 3.

   b. Pull the thread across the surface, enter at 9 and exit at 2. Pull the thread to form the eye lines and lock at 2.

   c. To form the mouth, reenter at 2 and exit at 10. Pull the thread across the surface, enter at 11 and exit at 2. Pull the thread firmly until the mouth line appears. Lock the stitch at 2.

   d. To form the bottom lip, reenter at 2 and exit at 12. Enter just barely to the left of 12 and exit at 3. Pull the thread firmly until the bottom lip appears and lock at 3.

   e. Reenter at 3, exit at 1, lock the stitch and cut the thread.

5. Cut another length of heavy-duty thread to sculpt the ears. Follow the entry and exit points illustrated in **Figure L**.

   a. Enter at 1, push the needle through the head and exit at 13. (Point 13, which will be the top of the ear, should be even with the bridge of the nose.) Pinch up a small curved ridge at an angle, as shown, just below point 13.

   b. Stitch back and forth underneath the ridge, moving toward point 14 with each stitch and pulling the thread gently until an ear forms. Exit at 14 and lock the stitch.

   c. Reenter at 14, exit at 1, lock and cut the thread.

   d. Repeat sub-steps a through c on the opposite side of the head to form the second ear.

6. Trim the blonde wiglet to fit Victoria's head and glue or stitch it in place. Comb the hair upward, arranging it in a bun of curls. Secure, using blonde hairpins.

7. Follow the illustration in **Figure M** to paint Victoria's eyes and lips. (See Tips & Techniques on fabric painting.) Paint a

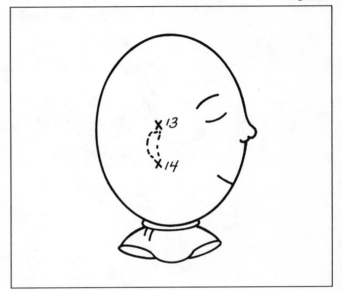

Figure N

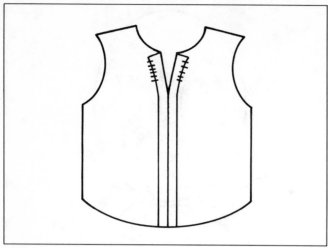

Figure O

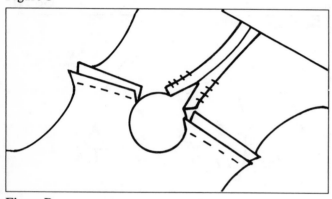

Figure P

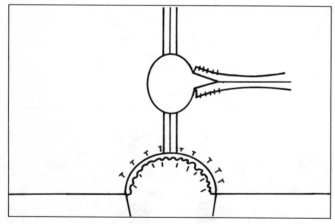

9. Turn a narrow seam allowance to the inside around the neck opening of the body. Run a line of basting stitches around the neckline ¼ inch from the folded edge, using heavy-duty flesh-tone thread. Pull the thread to gather the opening until it measures approximately 1 inch in diameter.

10. Center the head over the opening and insert the tied neck portion inside the body. Position the head so the nose points slightly upward. (Victoria finds it necessary to look down her nose quite frequently!) Whipstitch completely around the neck several times to secure the head to the body.

Making the Blouse

1. Place the two Blouse Backs right sides together. Stitch the center back seam from the lower edge to the small circle, leaving the upper portion of the seam open. Press the seam open. Turn the raw edges under along the unstitched portion of the seam and whipstitch in place (**Figure N**).

2. Pin the Blouse Front and the blouse back assembly right sides together along the shoulder seams (**Figure O**). Stitch the shoulder seams and press open.

3. Run a line of basting stitches along the top of one Sleeve, ⅜ inch from the raw edge, between the small circles. Pull the thread to gather the top of the Sleeve. Pin the gathered edge of the Sleeve to one armhole edge of the blouse, placing right sides together and adjusting the gathers evenly (**Figure P**). Stitch the seam along the gathering line. Clip the curve and turn the sleeve outward. Press the seam allowances toward the blouse. Attach the remaining Sleeve to the opposite armhole edge of the blouse in the same manner.

4. Fold the blouse right sides together and stitch the underarm and side seams (**Figure Q**).

5. Pin the 6-inch length of satin-and-lace trim lengthwise along the center front of the blouse. Topstitch close to the edges of the satin.

6. To finish the neckline, turn under and topstitch a ¼-inch hem. Topstitch the gold-and-lace neckline trim over the hemmed edge.

7. To make a casing for elastic at the lower edge of one sleeve, first press the seam allowance to the inside. Turn under a 1-inch hem and stitch close to the pressed edge, leaving a small opening to insert the elastic. Stitch again ⅜ inch from the first stitching, as shown in **Figure R**.

8. Measure Victoria's wrist and cut a piece of elastic 1 inch longer. Thread the elastic through the casing. Stitch together the ends of the elastic and pull them back inside the casing. Whipstitch the opening in the casing.

9. Repeat steps 7 and 8 to finish the second sleeve.

10. Dress Victoria in the blouse so that it can be fitted to her waistline. Divide the excess fabric at the waist into six equal front pleats, placing three pleats on each side of the center trim (**Figure S**). Baste the pleats in place and the fitting is complete.

Making the Skirt and Slip

1. Fold the Skirt widthwise, with right sides together, and stitch the center back seam. Press the seam open. Turn under and stitch a 1½-inch hem around the lower edge (**Figure T**).

small, softly edged triangle of white along the upper edge of each eye line. When the white paint has dried completely, add a small black circle in the center of the white. Paint a short, solid black line over the top of the circle and lightly brush black over the entire upper edge of the white triangle, widening it over the outer corner of the eye. Paint small arched eyebrows. (For some inexplicable reason, although Victoria's hair is naturally blonde, she has black eyebrows.)

8. Paint small red heart-shaped lips. Pat a little cosmetic blusher across Victoria's cheeks to give her a rosy glow.

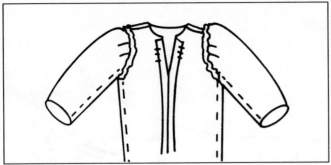

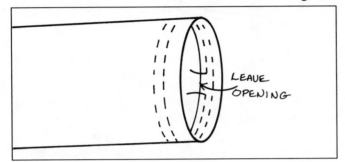

LEAVE OPENING

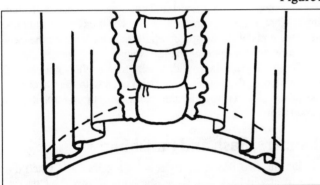

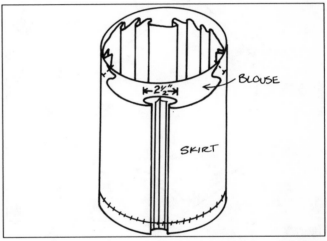

BLOUSE

SKIRT

2½"

Figure V

2. Victoria's skirt is fitted flat across the front and it is pleated and gathered in the back. Pin the center front of the skirt to the center front of the blouse, placing right sides together. Pin the skirt flat against the blouse front, working around to the side seams of the blouse. Fold a 2½-inch-wide double pleat at the center back of the skirt, as shown in **Figure U**.

3. Run a line of basting stitches close to the edge of the skirt waistline between the double pleat and the side seam of the blouse on each side. Ease the gathers to fit, as shown in **Figure V**. Stitch the skirt to the blouse all the way around.

4. Turn the skirt and blouse right side out and press the waistline seam allowances toward the skirt. To create the swagged hemline (**Figure W**), baste from the bottom of the hem halfway up the left side of the skirt. Pull the basting thread to gather the skirt gently and take another small stitch to anchor it in place. Tie the 1-inch-wide white satin ribbon into a bow and tack it to the skirt at the top of the gathers.

5. Fold the Slip widthwise, with right sides together, and stitch the center back seam. Press the seam open. To make a casing for elastic at the waist, turn under and stitch a ½-inch

Figure W

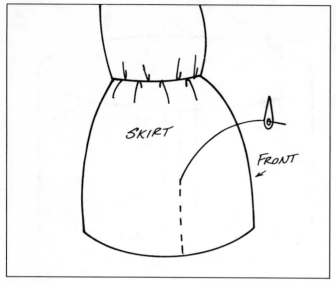

Figure X

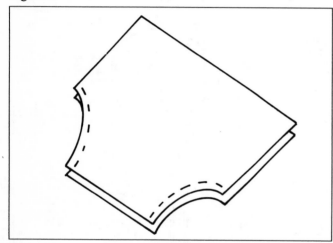

Figure Y

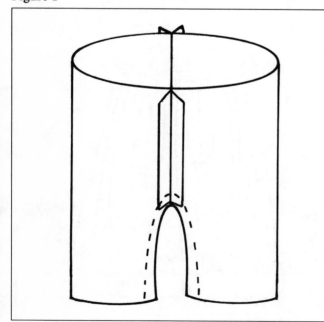

Figure Z

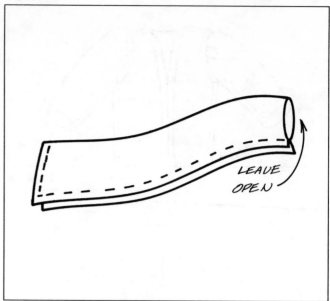

hem around the top of the slip. Leave a small opening in the stitching to insert the elastic.

6. Measure Victoria's waist and cut a piece of elastic 1 inch longer. Thread the elastic through the waist casing. Stitch together the ends of the elastic and pull them back inside the casing. Whipstitch the opening in the casing.

7. Topstitch the 5-inch-wide eyelet trim to the right side of the slip, placing the bottom of the trim even with the lower raw edge of the slip. Trim away the excess taffeta underneath the stitched trim.

Bloomers, Sash and Finishing

1. Pin the two Bloomers right sides together and stitch the center front and back seams, as shown in **Figure X**. Clip the curves and press the seams open.

2. Refold the bloomers so the center front seam matches the center back seam and the legs are even. Stitch the inner leg seam (**Figure Y**). Clip the curves and press the seam open.

3. Make casings at the waist and leg edges of the bloomers, as you did for the sleeves and slip. Measure and cut lengths of elastic and thread them through the casings.

4. Topstitch lace trim around the lower finished edges of the bloomer legs.

5. Fold the taffeta Sash lengthwise, with right sides together. Stitch the seam along the long edge and one end, leaving the other end open, as shown in **Figure Z**.

6. Turn the sash right side out and press. Turn the raw edges to the inside at the open end and whipstitch.

7. Dress Victoria in her bloomers and slip. Sew the hook-and-eye closure to the back neckline of the blouse. Without mussing Vicki's (oops!) Victoria's coiffure, slip the blouse and skirt over her head. Tie the sash around her waist, ending with a soft double knot at the back. Blouse out the front of her bodice. (Although nature was certainly not generous with Victoria in this department, she accentuates what she does have.) Glue or sew the rhinestone earrings to Victoria's ear lobes.

Kim Sue, Muffy and Fredd Redd

Three times the fun! The same basic patterns and assembly techniques will produce all three of these adorable dolls. Kim Sue is our doll-baby ready for her nap; Muffy is all decked out in her lace-trimmed finery; and Fredd Redd is a red-and-white striped clown ready to tickle your funny bone! Each doll is approximately 18 inches tall.

Materials

For Kim Sue:

¾ yard of 36-inch-wide pink flannel for the sleeper
4-inch square of long black fur fabric for the hair
1-yard length of yarn or narrow ribbon that coordinates with the sleeper fabric

For Muffy:

½ yard of 36-inch white organdy for the underskirt and apron
½ yard of 36-inch lightweight cotton for the skirt and hat lining (We used peach-colored fabric.)
½ yard of cotton duck for the legs (We used a striped fabric in coordinating colors.)
9 x 12-inch piece of heavy-weight fabric for the hat brim (We used upholstery fabric in a coordinating color.)
9 x 12-inch piece of fusible interfacing
½ yard of calico for the arms and torso
5 x 15-inch piece of brown fleece for the shoes
1 yard of 1-inch white lace trim
1 yard of ½-inch white lace trim
1½ yards of 1-inch white eyelet trim
¾ yard of ½-inch white satin ribbon
¾ yard of ¼-inch satin ribbon in a color that coordinates with the fabrics
One skein of light yellow rug yarn for the hair
12-inch length of ¼-inch elastic

For Fredd Redd:

¾ yard of red-and-white striped cotton for the body
3 yards of ¼-inch white satin ribbon
⅛ yard of red-and-white polka-dot fabric for the collar
3½ x 24-inch piece of solid red fabric for the collar
Half skein of light yellow rug yarn (We used the same color for Muffy and Fredd Redd.)

For *each* doll:

¼ yard of flesh-tone fleece for the head, hands and feet
Half bag of polyester fiberfill
Long sharp needle; and flesh-tone heavy-duty thread
Regular sewing needle; and regular thread to match the fabrics
Hot-melt glue and a glue gun (or white glue)
Cosmetic cheek blusher
Non-toxic felt-tip marking pens in red and black
Embroidery floss in red and brown

Cutting the Pieces

1. Full-size patterns are provided in **Figure A** for the Hand and Foot. (Notations on the patterns indicate which patterns belong to which doll.) Trace the patterns.

2. Scale drawings are provided in **Figure B** for the Shoe, Bonnet, Torso, Hat and Head. (Notations on the drawings indicate which pieces belong to which doll.) Enlarge the drawings to make full-size paper patterns. (See Tips & Techniques.)

3. Cut the pieces as listed in this step from the specified fabric types and colors.

Kim Sue:

Flannel:
    Arm – cut two, 7 x 11 inches
    Leg – cut two, 8½ x 11 inches
    Torso – cut two

Fleece:
    Head – cut two
    Hand – cut four
    Foot – cut four

Muffy:

Fleece:
    Head – cut two
    Hand – cut four

Organdy:
    Apron – cut one, 7½ x 17 inches
    Underskirt – cut one, 9 x 34 inches

Calvert City Public Library
Calvert City, Kentucky

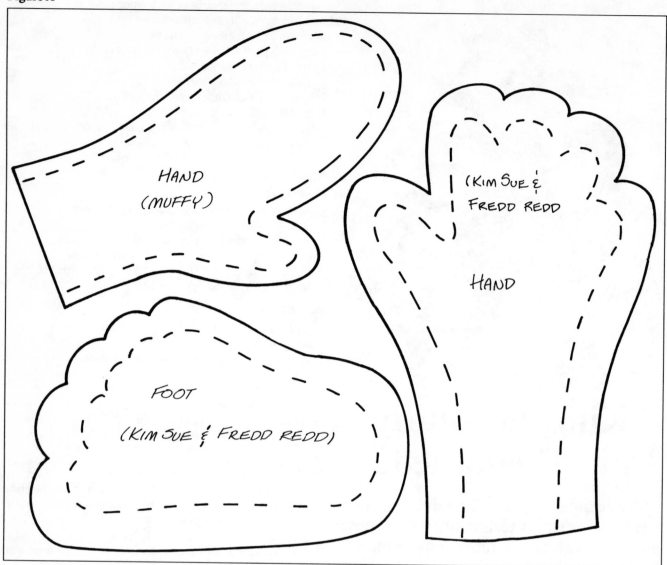

Calico:
  Torso – cut two
  Arm – cut two, 8½ x 13 inches
Cotton duck:
  Leg – cut two, 11 x 17 inches
Upholstery fabric:
  Bonnet – cut one
Peach-colored cotton:
  Skirt – cut one, 10 x 34 inches
  Bonnet Lining – cut one
Brown Fleece:
  Shoe – cut four
Fredd Redd:
  Red-and-white:
  Leg – cut two, 11 x 17 inches
  Arm – cut two, 8½ x 13 inches
  Torso – cut two
  Hat – cut one

Fleece:
  Head – cut two
  Hand – cut four
  Foot – cut four

General Information

Basic construction of these dolls is quite simple. The arms and legs are lightly stuffed rectangles of fabric with both ends gathered. One gathered end is sewn into the torso seam and the other is whipstitched to a hand or foot. The clothing serves as the body (except for Muffy's skirt and apron), so you don't have to make separate bodies and clothing to fit. All seams are ½-inch, unless otherwise specified.

KIM SUE

Legs, Arms and Torso

1. Turn under and stitch a ¼-inch hem along one 11-inch

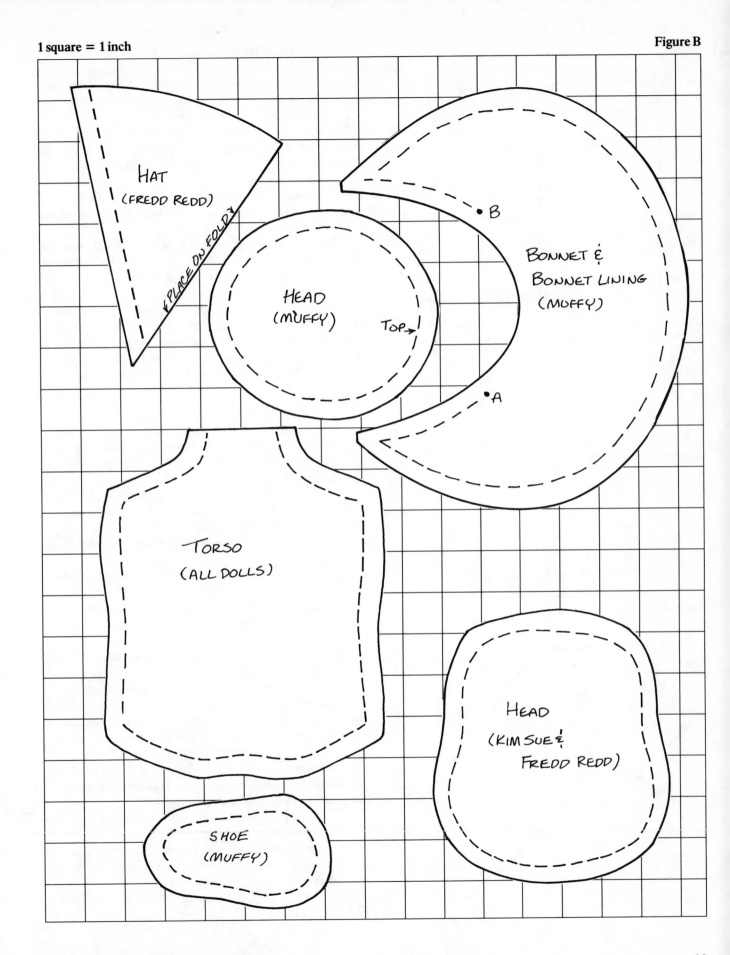

HAT
(FREDD REDD)

← PLACE ON FOLD →

HEAD
(MUFFY)

TOP →

• B

BONNET &
BONNET LINING
(MUFFY)

• A

TORSO
(ALL DOLLS)

HEAD
(KIM SUE &
FREDD REDD)

SHOE
(MUFFY)

Figure C

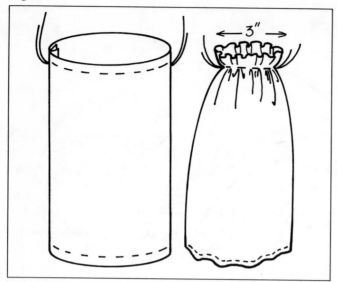

Figure D

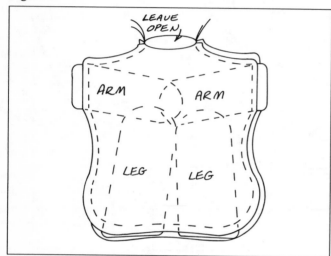

LEAVE OPEN

ARM   ARM

LEG   LEG

Figure E

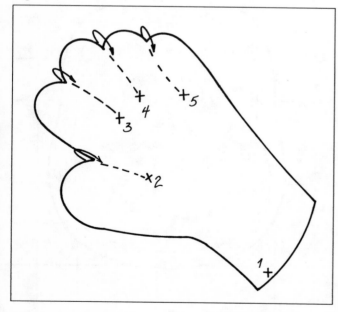

edge of one Leg (**Figure C**). Fold the Leg in half widthwise, with right sides together, and stitch the seam along the 8¼-inch edge. Press the seam open. You should now have a tube with one end hemmed. Turn the leg tube right side out. Assemble a second leg tube in the same manner.

2. Flatten the leg tube with the seam at one side. Baste through both layers about ½ inch from the unhemmed edge. Gather the leg until it is 3 inches wide (**Figure C**). Gather the other leg in the same manner.

3. The arms are formed in the same manner as the legs. Repeat steps 1 and 2 for each arm, gathering the unhemmed end until it is 2 inches wide.

4. Place an arm on the right side of one Torso (**Figure D**), aligning the gathered end with one armhole edge of the Torso. Baste in place along the seam line. Baste the second arm and both legs to the Torso in the same manner.

5. Place the second Torso right side down on top of the stack. (The arms and legs will be sandwiched between.) Stitch the Torso seams (**Figure D**), leaving the neck open. Be careful that you don't catch any of the lower arm and leg material in the seams. Clip the curves and corners and turn right side out.

Hands and Feet

1. Place two Hands right sides together and stitch the seam, leaving the wrist open. Clip the curves and corners, turn right side out and stuff with fiberfill. Whipstitch the wrist opening. Make a second hand in the same manner.

2. Soft-sculpt the fingers on each hand, using flesh-tone heavy-duty thread and a long sharp needle and following the entry and exit points illustrated in **Figure E**.

    a. Enter at 1 on the wrist, push the needle through the hand and exit at 2.

    b. To form the thumb, take small stitches back and forth through the hand, working out to the end.

    c. Wrap the thread around the end of the hand, enter on the back, push the needle through the hand and exit at 3 on the front.

    d. To form the fingers, repeat sub-steps b and c at points 3, 4 and 5. Lock the stitch at 5 and cut the thread.

3. Place two Feet right sides together and stitch the seam around the edge, leaving an opening at the heel. Clip the curves and turn right side out. Press the seam allowances to the inside along the opening. Stuff with fiberfill and blindstitch the opening. Make a second foot in the same manner.

4. Soft-sculpt the toes on each foot, using flesh-tone heavy-duty thread and a long sharp needle and following the entry and exit points illustrated in **Figure F**.

    a. Enter at point 1 on the bottom of the foot and exit at point 1 on the top.

    b. To form the big toe, wrap the thread around the end of the foot, enter at 1 on the back and exit at 1 on the top. Pull the thread to separate the toes.

    c. Reenter at 1, push the needle through the foot and exit at 2 on the top.

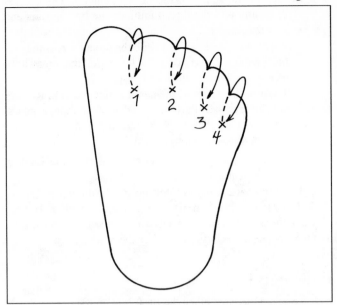

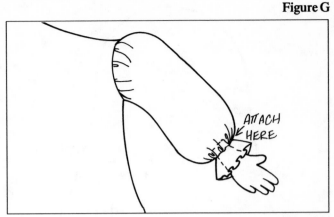

ATTACH HERE

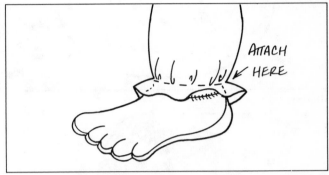

ATTACH HERE

d. Repeat sub-steps b and c at points 2, 3 and 4 to form the other toes. Lock the stitch at 4 and cut the thread.

5. To attach the hands, first insert a fist-sized ball of fiberfill inside one arm. Do not stuff the arm tightly. Run a line of basting stitches around the lower end of the stuffed arm about ½ inch from the hemmed edge. Don't cut off the tails of thread. Insert the wrist, making sure that the thumb points upward. Pull the basting threads to gather the arm fabric around the wrist, as shown in **Figure G**. Tie off the gathers and whipstitch the arm to the hand. Attach the second hand in the same manner.

6. Insert a slightly larger ball of fiberfill inside one leg. Again, do not stuff the leg tightly. Gather the hemmed edge of the leg in the same manner as you did the arms. Whipstitch the leg to the top of the foot, as shown in **Figure H**. Attach the second foot in the same manner.

Assembling the Head

1. Cut a small hole just below the center of one Head piece, as shown in **Figure I**. This will be the Head Back (the neck will be inserted into this hole later).

2. Place the Head and Head Back right sides together and stitch the seam all the way around the edge. Clip the curves and turn the head right side out through the hole in the Head Back. Stuff with fiberfill.

3. Cut a 1½-inch-diameter circle of fleece for the nose. Run a line of basting stitches close to the outer edge. Place a small ball of fiberfill in the center, on the wrong side of the fabric, and pull the threads to gather the fabric around the stuffing, as shown in **Figure J**.

4. Slightly flatten the nose and place the gathered edge against the face. Blindstitch the nose to the face, as shown in **Figure K**. Soft-sculpt the rest of the facial features, using a long sharp needle and flesh-tone heavy-duty thread and following the entry and exit points shown in **Figure K**.

    a. To form the eyes, enter at 1 on the back of the head. Push the needle through the head and exit at 2.

Figure I

HEAD BACK

CUT OUT

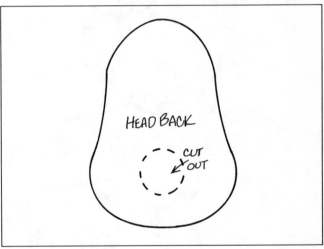

Figure K

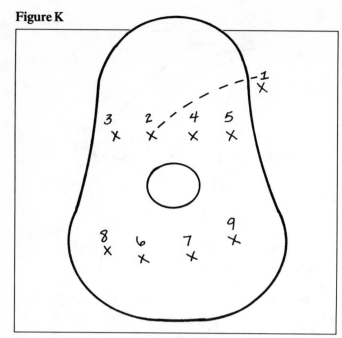

Figure L

Figure M

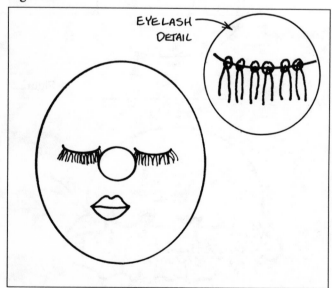

EYELASH DETAIL

b. Pull the thread across the surface, enter at 3 and exit at 2. Gently pull the thread until an eye line appears and lock the stitch at 2.

c. Reenter at 2 and exit at 4. Pull the thread across the surface, enter at 5 and exit at 2. Gently pull the thread until an eye line appears and lock the stitch at 2.

d. To form the dimples, reenter at 2 and exit at 8. Reenter at 8 and exit at 2. Pull the thread until a dimple appears. Reenter at 2 and exit at 9. Reenter at 9 and exit at 2. Pull the thread and lock the stitch at 2.

e. To form the mouth, reenter at 2 and exit at 6. Enter at 7 and exit at 2. Pull and lock the thread.

f. Reenter at 2, exit at 1, lock and cut the thread.

5. To attach the head, insert the neck into the back of the head through the hole. Turn the raw edge of the opening to the inside, clipping where necessary. Whipstitch the head to the neck.

Finishing Touches

1. To make the hair, place the fur fabric on Kim Sue's head, positioning it as it looks best to you. Trim the shape as you like. Secure it with glue or whipstitches. Brush or comb the hair over the head.

2. To finish Kim Sue's face (**Figure L**), apply a little blusher to her cheeks, nose and chin. You can add color to her mouth, using a red felt-tip marker or blusher. Draw a dark line across each eye line, using a black marker.

3. Tie lengths of yarn or ribbon around her wrists, neck and ankles. Make a small bow and attach it to her head.

MUFFY

Making the Body

1. Refer to the "Legs, Arms and Torso" section for Kim Sue and assemble Muffy's body in the same manner, with the following exceptions:

    a. Hem one 17-inch edge for each Leg.

    b. Hem one 13-inch edge for each Arm.

    c. Stitch ½-inch white lace trim to the hemmed edge of each arm.

2. Refer to the "Hands and Feet" section and assemble and soft-sculpt Muffy's hands in the same manner.

3. Muffy has stuffed shoes instead of feet. Stitch the Shoes together in the same manner as you did Kim Sue's feet. Attach the hands and shoes in the same manner.

4. Refer to "Assembling the Head" and follow the instructions through step 4 to assemble and soft-sculpt Muffy's head and nose.

5. **Figure M** shows Muffy's face. Use red embroidery floss and work satin stitches to form her mouth. Long, luxurious brown lashes frame her closed eyes. Work about six knotted stitches along each eye line (**Figure M**, inset).

6. Attach Muffy's head as you did Kim Sue's.

7. To make Muffy's hair, cut about ninety 22-inch strands of light yellow rug yarn. Place the center of the bundle across the top center of Muffy's head, as shown in **Figure N**. Tack the cen-

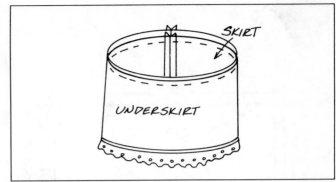

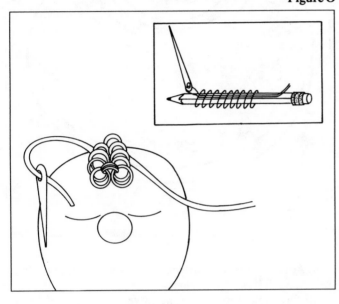

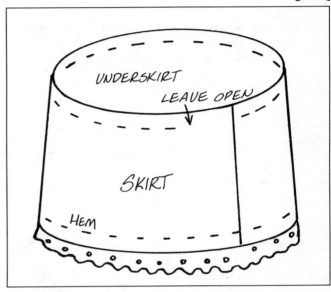

ter of the bundle to the head, using heavy-duty thread. Tie a 12-inch length of ½-inch white satin ribbon around each side to form loose pony tails, as shown.

8. Muffy has cute little curls for bangs. Thread a needle with heavy-duty thread and use a continuous length of rug yarn. Tack one end of the yarn to the top of her head at the front. Do not cut the thread. Wrap the yarn around a pencil four or five times (**Figure O**, inset) and slip the needle between the yarn and pencil. Slide the curls off the pencil and tack in place (**Figure O**). Continue with the same lengths of yarn and thread, making as many curls as you want in the same manner. Cut the yarn and tack the end underneath a curl.

Skirt, Apron and Bonnet

1. Turn under and stitch a narrow hem along one 34-inch edge of both the Skirt and the Underskirt. Stitch the 1-inch white lace edging to the hemmed edge of the Underskirt.

2. Fold the Skirt right sides together and stitch the side seam. Stitch the side seam on the Underskirt in the same manner. Press the seams open.

3. Place the Skirt and Underskirt right sides together (**Figure P**), matching the raw waist edges. Stitch close to the raw edges,

as shown. Turn the skirts with wrong sides together and press the seam.

4. To make a casing, topstitch ½ inch from the waist seam (**Figure Q**), leaving an opening at the side seams. Thread the length of elastic through the casing, whipstitch the ends of the elastic together and slip them back inside the casing. Whipstitch the opening.

5. Hem the skirt short enough for the lace trim to peek out beneath the hem, as shown in **Figure Q**. Place the skirt-and-underskirt assembly on Muffy.

6. To prepare the Apron, round off the two corners at the ends of one long edge (**Figure R**). These will be the lower corners. Stitch eyelet trim along the entire contoured edge, but not along the straight top edge, as shown. Baste close to the straight edge and gather to 6 inches in length. Tie off the basting threads.

7. Fold the Apron Tie in half lengthwise with right sides together. Cut the ends at an angle (**Figure S**, diagram 1). Stitch, leaving a 6-inch opening at the center. Turn right side out and press the seam allowances to the inside along the opening.

8. Place the gathered edge of the apron inside the opening in the apron tie. Topstitch the seam, as shown in **Figure S**, diagram 2. Tie the apron around Muffy's waist on top of her skirt.

Figure R

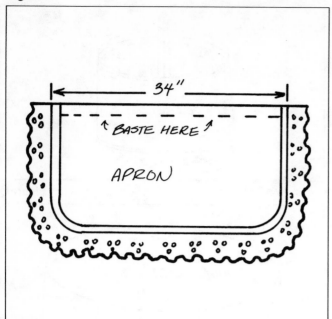

Figure S

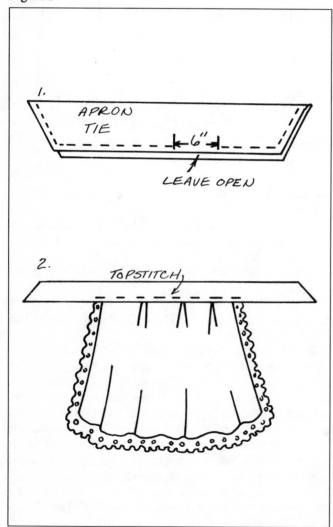

Figure T

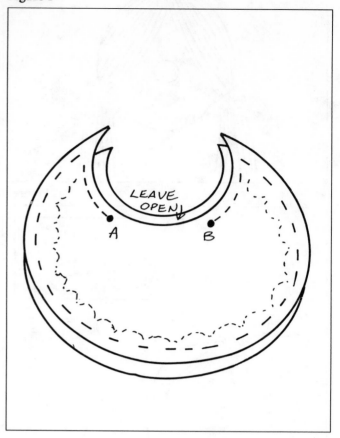

9. Attach the fusible interfacing to the *wrong* side of the Bonnet Lining, following the manufacturer's instructions.

10. Pin eyelet trim around the curved outer edge of the unlined Bonnet (**Figure T**), matching raw edges. Place the Bonnet Lining right side down on top (the eyelet will be sandwiched between). Stitch around the edge, beginning at point **A** and ending at point **B**. Clip the curves and corners and turn right side out. Press the seam allowances to the inside and blindstitch the opening. Cut the ¼-inch satin ribbon in half. Fold over and tack one end to each corner of the bonnet.

FREDD REDD

1. Refer to the "Legs, Arms and Torso" section for Kim Sue and assemble Fredd's body in the same manner, with the following exceptions:

    a. Hem one 17-inch edge for each leg.

    b. Hem one 13-inch edge of each arm.

2. Refer to the "Hands and Feet" section and assemble and soft-sculpt Fredd's hands and feet in the same manner.

3. Refer to "Assembling the Head" and follow the same instructions, omitting the dimples. Attach the head to the body in the same manner. Use generous amounts of cosmetic blusher for Fredd's rosy cheeks, nose and chin. You can use felt-tip markers in red for the mouth and black for the eye lines, or you can use embroidery floss and work the mouth and eyes in the same manner as you did for Muffy.

4. Fredd's hair (**Figure U**) is attached around the crown of

Figure V

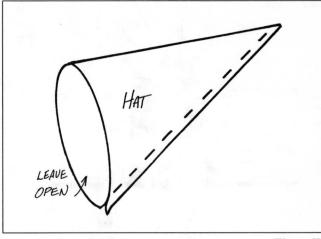

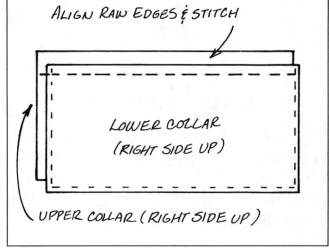

Figure X

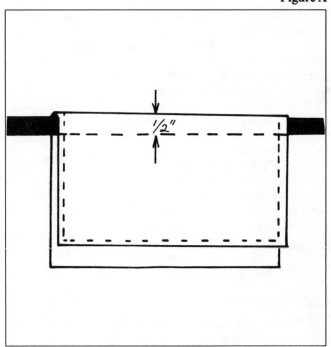

his head and then cut at uneven lengths. His hat covers the bald spot, with hair sticking out from underneath. To make Fredd's hair, cut 10-inch strands of rug yarn and separate them into bunches of four or five strands. Fold in half and tack the center of each bunch to his head, as shown. Do not attach any hair to the top of his head. Trim the strands at uneven lengths.

5. To assemble Fredd's hat (**Figure V**), fold the Hat right sides together, stitch the long straight seam and press open. Turn under and stitch a ¼-inch hem around the lower edge. Blindstitch the hat to Fredd's head. Bend the tip over to one side and tack it to the hat. You can attach a small pompom or white ribbon bow to the tip of his hat.

6. Fredd wears a ruffled double collar. The lower layer is red-and-white polka-dot fabric and the upper layer is solid red. Turn under and stitch a narrow hem along both ends and one long edge of the Upper Collar. Hem the Lower Collar in the same manner. Stack the Upper and Lower Collars, both right side up, aligning the raw edges and with the Lower Collar on top. Stitch a ¼-inch seam along the edge, as shown in **Figure W**, and press open. Fold the Upper Collar over the Lower Collar (the right side of each should be facing the same direction) and press.

7. To make a casing (**Figure X**), topstitch about ½ inch below the seam line. Thread a 24-inch length of white ribbon through the casing. Gather the collar along the ribbon and wrap it around Fredd's neck. Tie the ribbon in a big bow.

8. Tie lengths of ribbon around Fredd's wrists and ankles.

Big Hoppy

Even though Big Hoppy stands 5 feet 8 inches tall, he's still cute and huggable. His soft-sculpted facial features and larger-than-life-size body make him one of a kind in the rabbit world.

Materials

2½ yards of white medium-weight poly-cotton fabric (at least 45 inches wide), for the body
½ yard of pink poly-cotton for the ears and paw-pads
½ yard of green felt for the vest
12-inch square of pink felt for the eyelids and flower
Small piece of black felt for the eyes
6 x 30-inch piece of cotton print in a color that coordinates with the green and pink felt, for the bow tie
One 2-inch pink pompom for the nose
1 yard of pink yarn for the whiskers
Five bags of polyester fiberfill
White heavy-duty thread; and regular thread
Long sharp needle; and regular sewing needle
Small piece of thin white plastic or cardboard for the teeth
Cosmetic cheek blusher
Hot-melt glue and a glue gun (or white glue)
Two coat hangers (or medium-weight wire) for the ears
Small amount of adhesive tape

Cutting the Pieces

1. Full-size patterns are provided in **Figure A** for the Teeth, Eye, Eyelid and Small Paw-Pad. Trace the patterns.

Figure A

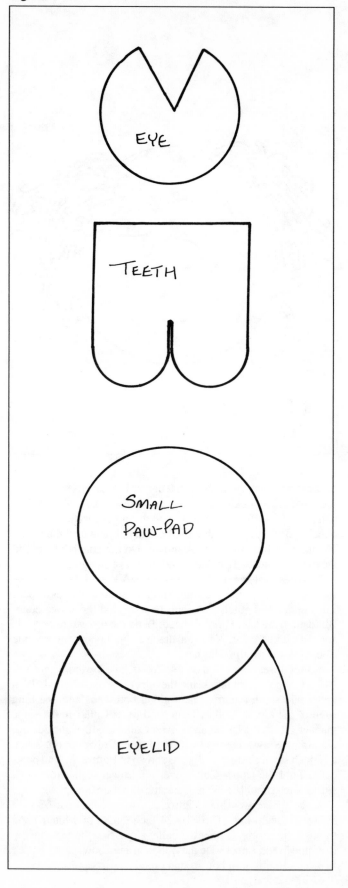

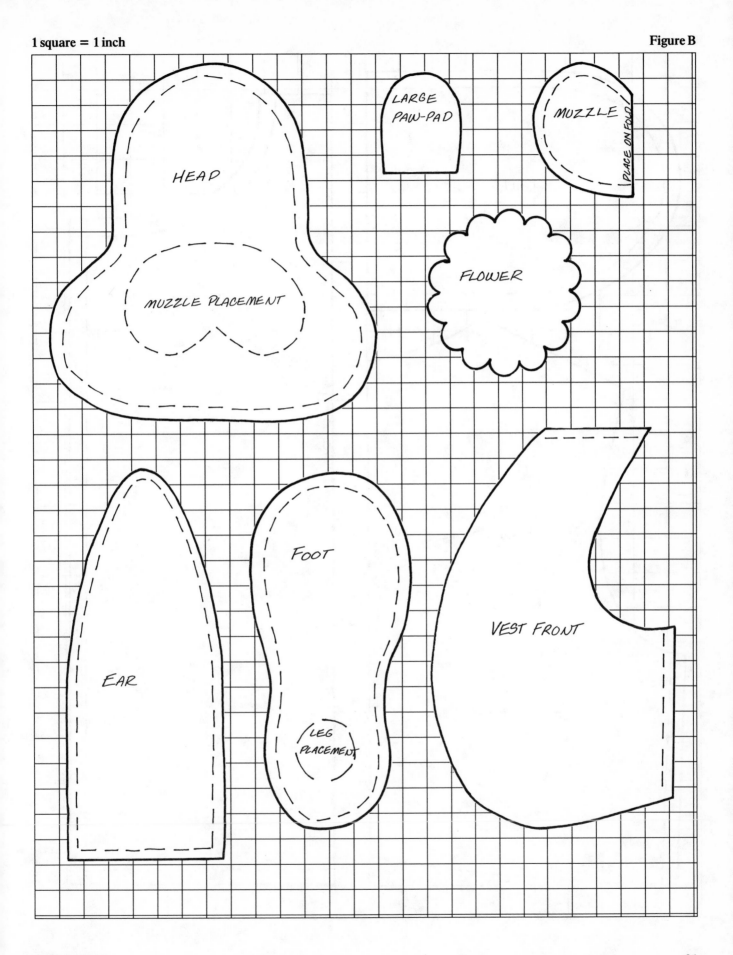

HEAD

MUZZLE PLACEMENT

LARGE PAW-PAD

MUZZLE

PLACE ON FOLD

FLOWER

EAR

FOOT

LEG PLACEMENT

VEST FRONT

Figure C 1 square = 1 inch

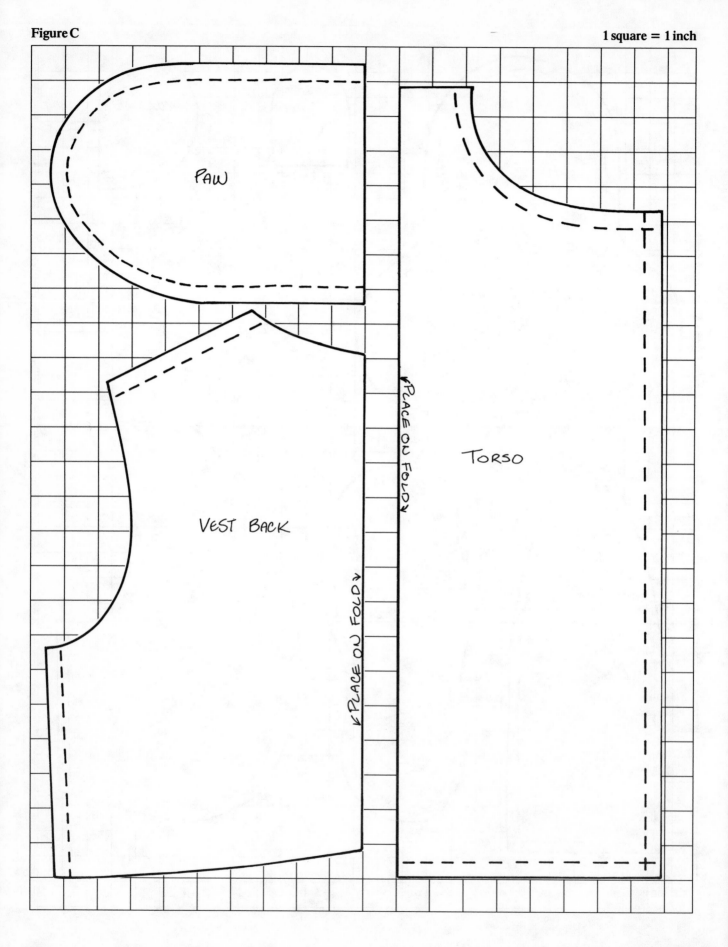

PAW

VEST BACK

TORSO

PLACE ON FOLD

PLACE ON FOLD

2. Scale drawings are provided in **Figures B** and **C** for the Torso, Flower, Vest Front, Vest Back, Ear, Head, Large Paw-Pad, Muzzle, Paw and Foot. Enlarge the drawings to make full-size paper patterns. (See Tips & Techniques.)

3. Cut the pieces as listed in this step from the specified fabric types and colors.

White poly-cotton:
    Torso – cut two
    Arm – cut two, 13 x 21 inches
    Leg – cut two, 13 x 28 inches
    Paw – cut four
    Head – cut two
    Ear – cut two
    Foot – cut four
    Muzzle – cut two

Pink poly-cotton:
    Ear – cut two
    Large Paw-Pad – cut four
    Small Paw-Pad – cut twelve
    Chest Oval – cut one, 10 x 16 inches

Pink felt:
    Flower – cut one
    Eyelid – cut two

Green felt:
    Vest Front – cut two
    Vest Back – cut one

Black felt:
    Eye – cut two

White plastic:
    Teeth – cut one

Making the Arms, Legs and Torso

The arms and legs are stitched rectangles of fabric that are stuffed after they are attached to the torso. One end is sewn into the torso seam and the other is whipstitched to a paw or foot.

1. Fold one Arm in half lengthwise, placing right sides together, so you have a rectangle that measures 6½ x 21 inches. Stitch the seam along the long edge, leaving both ends open. Turn the arm right side out. Make another arm in the same manner, using the remaining Arm piece.

2. Fold one Leg in half lengthwise, placing right sides together, so you have a rectangle that measures 6½ x 28 inches. Stitch the seam along the long edge, leaving both ends open. Turn the leg right side out. Make another leg in the same manner, using the remaining Leg piece.

3. Choose one Torso as the front and applique the pink Chest Oval to it, as shown in **Figure D**. Set the appliqued Front Torso aside for the moment.

4. Place the Back (undecorated) Torso right side up on a flat surface. Place an arm on top, aligning one end with the armhole edge (**Figure E**). Be sure the folded edge of the arm is nearest the shoulder edge. Baste the arm in place along the seam line. Repeat for the second arm.

5. Fold one leg tube so that the seam is centered and place it on top of the Back Torso (**Figure F**), aligning one end with the leg edge. Baste the leg in place along the seam line. Repeat for the second leg.

Figure D

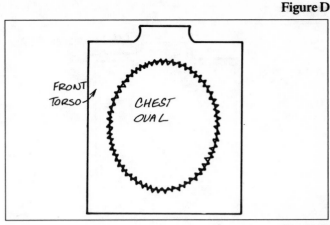

Figure E

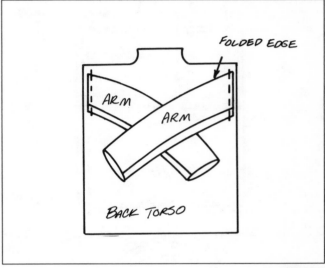

Figure F

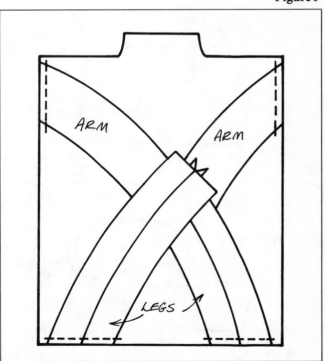

Figure G

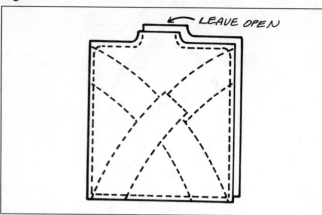

Figure H

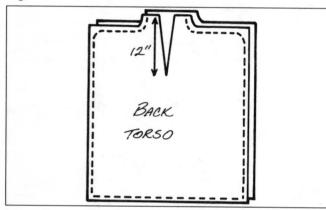

Figure I

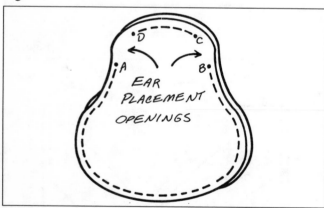

Figure J

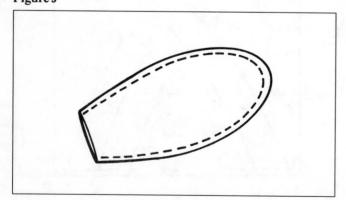

6. Place the appliqued Front Torso right side down on top of the stack, sandwiching the arms and legs between, as shown in **Figure G**. Stitch the seam around the edges of the Torso, leaving the neck open. (Be careful that you don't catch any of the lower arm or leg material in the seam.) Clip the curves and corners. Remove the basting threads.

7. As you have probably noticed, the neck opening is rather small. For ease in turning and stuffing the torso, enlarge the opening by cutting a slit in the Back Torso, starting at the neck edge and cutting downward about 12 inches (**Figure H**).

8. Turn the torso right side out through the opening. Stuff the torso fairly full with fiberfill and whipstitch the slit. Do not whipstitch the neck edges yet.

9. Stuff the arms and legs through the wrist and ankle openings. Do not whipstitch the openings.

Making the Head

1. Place the two Heads right sides together and stitch the contoured seam (**Figure I**), from A to B and then from C to D. Clip the curves and turn the head right side out through one of the ear placement openings. Stuff the head.

2. Place one pink Ear and one white Ear right sides together and stitch the long side seams (**Figure J**), leaving the short straight edge open. Clip the corner and curves and turn the ear right side out.

3. To make an ear support, bend a coat hanger (or wire) into the shape of the ear (**Figure K**). Wrap adhesive tape around the ends of the wire to prevent them from ripping the fabric. Insert the wire ear support inside the assembled ear.

4. Thread a long sharp needle with white heavy-duty thread and baste across the open edge of the ear. Pull the thread to gather the fabric so that it will fit inside one ear opening of the head. Insert the gathered edge into the opening, making sure the pink side faces forward. Blindstitch the opening.

5. Repeat steps 2 through 4 to assemble and attach the second ear, using the remaining pink and white Ear pieces.

6. Place the two Muzzles right sides together and stitch the contoured seam, leaving an opening, as shown in **Figure L**. Clip the curves and corner and turn the muzzle right side out. Lightly stuff the muzzle. Press the seam allowances to the inside and blindstitch the opening.

7. Place the muzzle against the front of the head (**Figure M**). The scalloped edge should be at the bottom. Pinch the sides of the muzzle toward each other so that the center humps upward along the lower edge. Whipstitch the muzzle to the head along the curved upper portion, leaving the lower scalloped edge unstitched, as shown.

8. Soft-sculpt the lower lip, using a long sharp needle and white heavy-duty thread and following the entry and exit points shown in **Figure M**.

    a. Pinch up a narrow curved ridge between point 1 and point 2.

    b. Enter at 1 and stitch back and forth underneath the ridge, exiting at point 2.

    c. Lock the stitch at point 2 and cut the thread.

9. **Figure N** shows the finished face. Glue the black felt Eyes in place. Glue the pink Eyelids in place, pinching the lower corners inward so the lids are raised. Glue the straight edge of the

Figure L

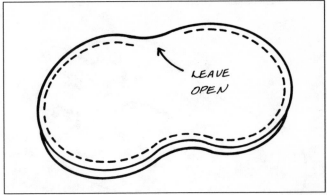

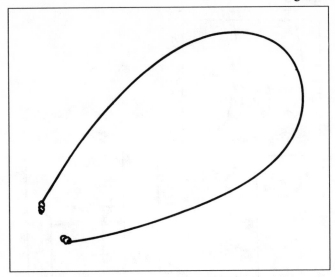

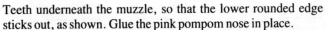

Teeth underneath the muzzle, so that the lower rounded edge sticks out, as shown. Glue the pink pompom nose in place.

10. To make the whiskers (**Figure N**), cut the pink yarn into six 6-inch strands. Tack the center of one yarn strand to the muzzle and tie the yarn in a knot, covering the tacking stitches. Repeat to attach three yarn whiskers on each side.

Making the Paws and Feet

1. Applique one Large Paw-Pad and three Small Paw-Pads to one Paw, as shown in **Figure O**. Applique a second Paw in the same manner.

2. Place one plain Paw and one appliqued Paw right sides together and stitch around the contoured edge, leaving the wrist open. Clip the curves, turn the paw right side out and stuff with fiberfill. Make a second paw in the same manner.

3. Soft-sculpt the toes, using a long sharp needle and white heavy-duty thread and following the entry and exit points shown in **Figure O**.

    a. Enter at 1 on the bottom (paw-pad side), push the needle through the paw and exit at 1 on the top.

    b. Wrap the thread around the end of the paw, enter at 1 on the bottom and exit at 1 on the top. Pull the thread tightly to divide the toe.

    c. Wrap the thread around the end of the paw again, entering at 1 on the bottom and exiting at 1 on the top. Pull the thread tightly and lock the stitch.

    d. Reenter at 1, push the needle through the paw and exit at 2 on the top.

    e. Wrap the thread around the end of the paw, enter at 2 on the bottom and exit at 2 on the top. Pull the thread to divide the toes.

    f. Wrap the thread around the end of the paw again, enter at 2 on the bottom and exit at 2 on the top. Reenter at 2, exit at 2 on the bottom, pull the thread, lock the stitch and cut the thread.

    g. Repeat sub-steps a through f to soft-sculpt the second paw in the same manner.

4. Applique one Large Paw-Pad and three Small Paw-Pads

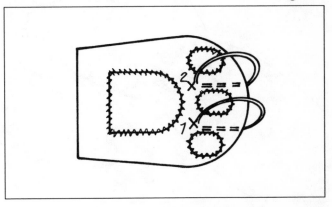

Figure P

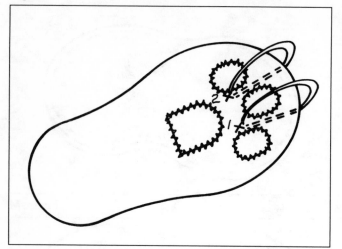

Figure Q

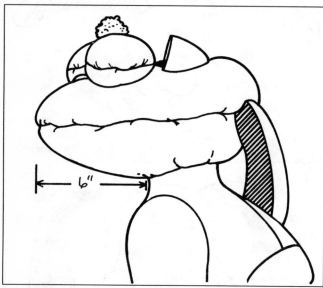

Figure R

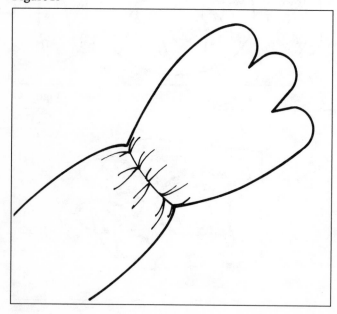

Figure S

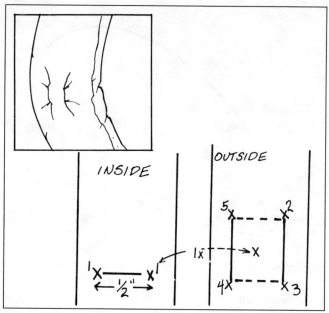

Figure T

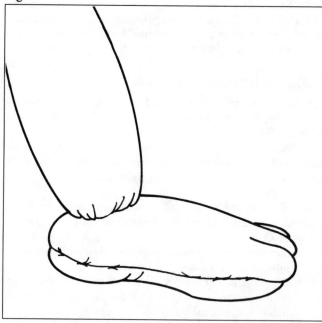

to one Foot, as shown in **Figure P**. Applique a second Foot in the same manner.

5. Place one plain Foot and one appliqued Foot right sides together and stitch around the contoured edge, leaving an opening at the heel. Clip the curves, turn the foot right side out and stuff fairly full with fiberfill. Press the seam allowances toward the inside and blindstitch the opening edges. Make a second foot in the same manner, using the remaining plain and appliqued Foot pieces.

6. To soft-sculpt the toes, repeat the procedures outlined in step 3 for the paws, following the entry and exit points illustrated in **Figure P**. Use a long sharp needle and heavy-duty white thread.

GREAT FABRIC DOLL BOOK

Attaching the Head, Paws and Feet

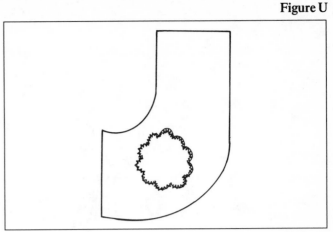

1. To attach the head (**Figure Q**), turn the torso seam allowance to the inside around the open neck edge. Place the head on top, with the face pointing upward. The neck should be about 6 inches behind the chin and the chin should point in the same direction as the front of the torso. Carefully bend Hoppy's head downward so his chin rests on his chest. (You will have to tuck the neck edge under a bit at the front to get this right.) Whipstitch around the neck several times to secure the head, starting at the center back.

2. To attach one paw **Figure R**, first press the seam allowance to the inside around the wrist edge. Insert the open end of the arm inside the paw and whipstitch (or blindstitch) the edges together, pulling and knotting the thread every three or four stitches to gather the wrist slightly. Attach the second paw in the same manner.

3. Soft-sculpt the elbow, using a long sharp needle and white heavy-duty thread and following the entry and exit points shown in **Figure S**.

> **a.** Enter at 1 on the inside of the elbow, push the needle through the arm and exit at 2 on the back.
>
> **b.** Pull the thread across the surface, enter at 3 and exit at point 4.
>
> **c.** Pull the thread across the surface, enter at 5 and exit at 2. Pull the thread until the elbow forms.
>
> **d.** Reenter at 2 and exit at 1. Enter about ½ inch to the side of 1 and exit at 1. Lock the stitch at 1 and cut the thread.
>
> **e.** Repeat sub-steps a through d to soft-sculpt the elbow on the second arm.

4. To attach one foot (**Figure T**), turn the seam allowance to the inside around the open leg edge. Whipstitch (or blindstitch) the leg to the top of the foot near the heel, as shown. Pull and knot the thread every three or four stitches to gather the ankle. Attach the second foot in the same manner.

5. The knees are formed in the same manner as the elbows. To soft-sculpt the knees, follow the procedures outlined in step 3 (and shown in **Figure S**), taking slightly larger stitches.

Making the Vest

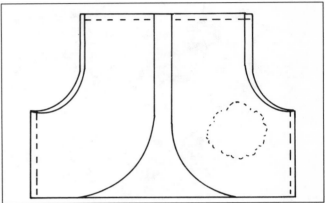

Figure V

1. Place the pink Flower right side up on the right side of one Vest Front (**Figure U**). Applique the Flower to the Vest.

2. Unfold the Vest Back and place it right side up on a flat surface. Place the Vest Fronts right side down on top, aligning the shoulder, side and armhole edges (**Figure V**). Stitch the shoulder and side seams, leaving the armhole edges open.

3. Press the seams and turn the vest right side out. Dress Hoppy in his sporty new vest.

4. Fold the 6 x 30-inch Tie in half lengthwise, placing right sides together. You should now have a rectangle that measures 3 x 30 inches. Stitch the seam along the long straight edge and one end, leaving the other end open. Clip the corners and turn the tie right side out. Press the seam allowances to the inside and whipstitch the opening edges together. Press the finished tie. Wrap it around Hoppy's neck and tie it in a knot. **Figure W** shows Hoppy finished, dressed and ready to go!

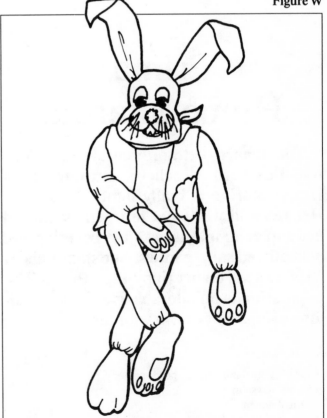

Prima Hippopotarina

Toe-dancer extraordinaire! You may find this hard to believe, but our Prima Hippopotarina is really light on her feet. Her red and white net tutu wraps around her rather ample waist, just covering her delicate red satin panties. She stands about 20 inches tall on her tippy-toes. Prima Hippopotarina is an adorable gift for the budding prima ballerina in your family.

Materials

½ yard of gray flannel for the head and body
½ yard of red satin
¼ yard of muslin
16 x 24-inch piece of red felt

Scraps of black and pink felt
1 yard of white bridal net
1 yard of red bridal net
½ yard of 1½-inch eyelet trim
2 yards of ½-inch red satin ribbon
1 yard of ¼-inch white satin ribbon
1 yard of red sequined ribbon
1 yard of red double-fold bias tape
Two small black buttons for the eyes
Two plastic eyelashes
One bag of polyester fiberfill
Long sharp needle; gray heavy-duty thread; and threads to match the fabrics
Hot-melt glue and a glue gun (or white glue)

Cutting the Pieces

1. Full-size patterns are provided in **Figure A** for the Paw, Ear, Ballet Shoe and Bodice. Trace the patterns.

2. Scale drawings are provided in **Figure B** for the Front Panty, Back Panty, Head, Arm and Body. Enlarge the drawings to make full-size paper patterns. (See Tips & Techniques.)

3. Cut the pieces as listed in this step from the specified types and colors of fabric.

Gray flannel:
    Head – cut one
    Ear – cut four
    Arm – cut two
    Paw – cut two
    Body – cut two
Red satin:
    Front Panty – cut one
    Back Panty – cut one
    Bodice – cut one
Muslin:
    Front Panty – cut one
    Back Panty – cut one
    Bodice – cut one
Red bridal net:
    Tutu – cut two, 10 x 36 inches
    Headpiece – cut one, 4 x 6 inches
White bridal net:
    Tutu – cut two, 10 x 36 inches
Red felt:
    Ballet Shoe – cut four

Making the Arms and Body

Note: All seam allowances are ⅜ inch unless otherwise specified in the instructions.

1. Fold one Arm in half lengthwise, placing right sides together. Stitch the seam along the long edge, stopping at the dot marked on the pattern. (The arm will be stuffed through this opening after it is attached to the body.) Leave both ends open. Press the seam allowances to the wrong side from the dot to the end of the arm.

2. Bast around one Paw, close to the edge. Pull the thread to gather, so the Paw will fit the smaller open end of the arm.

3. With right sides together, pin or baste the Paw to the small

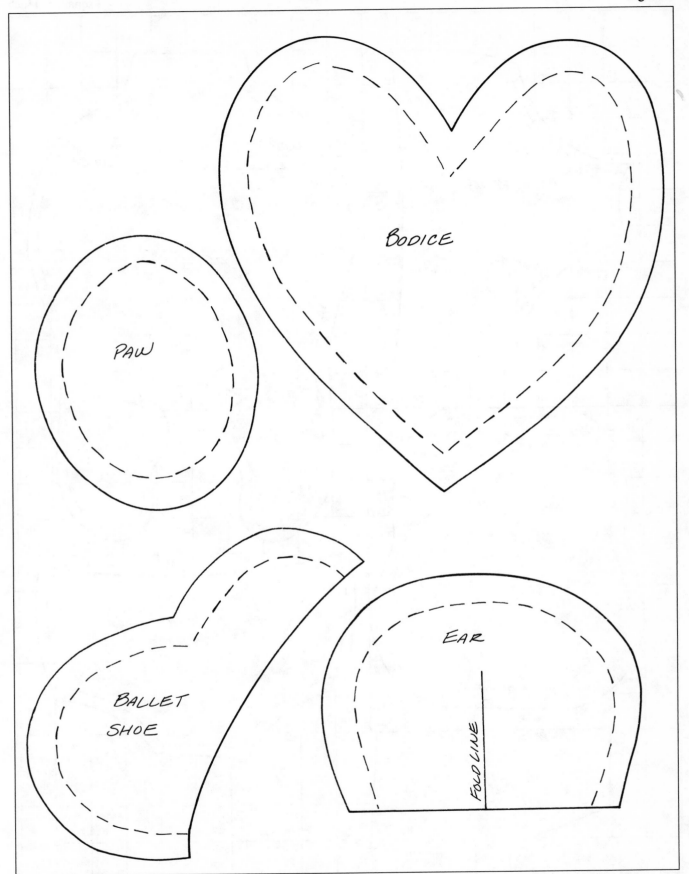

BODICE

PAW

BALLET SHOE

EAR

FOLD LINE

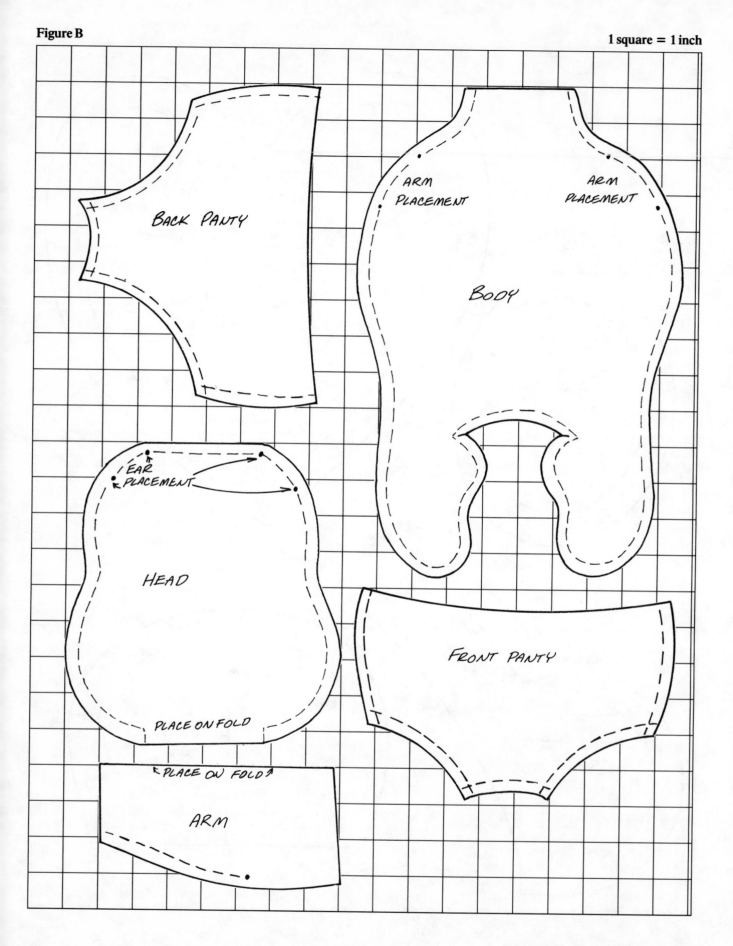

BACK PANTY

BODY

ARM
PLACEMENT

ARM
PLACEMENT

EAR
PLACEMENT

HEAD

FRONT PANTY

PLACE ON FOLD

PLACE ON FOLD

ARM

Figure C

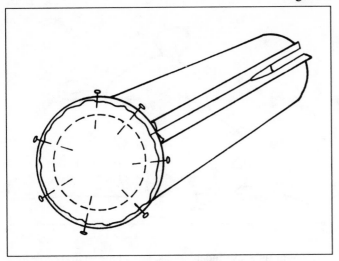

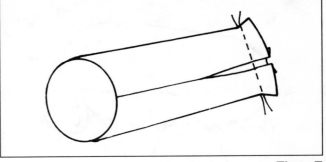

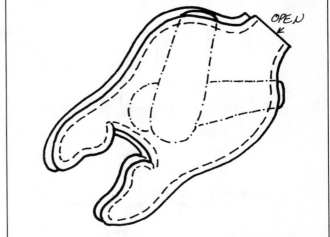

OPEN

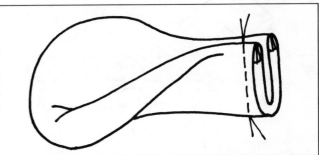

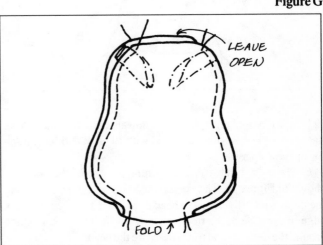

LEAVE OPEN

FOLD ↑

open end of the arm, as shown in **Figure C**. (You might need to readjust the gathers to fit the arm opening.) Stitch the seam, clip the curves and press the seam allowances toward the paw.

4. Turn the assembly right side out. Baste across the open end, as shown in **Figure D**.

5. Repeat steps 1 through 4 to make a second arm/paw assembly in the same manner.

6. Place one Body right side up on a flat surface. Place one arm/paw assembly on top between the placement marks indicated on the pattern, aligning the basted raw edge of the arm with the edge of the Body. Place the second arm along the opposite edge in the same manner.

7. Place the second Body right side down on top, sandwiching the two arm/paw assemblies between. Stitch the contoured seam, leaving the neck open, as shown in **Figure E**.

8. Clip the curves and corners and turn the body right side out. Press the allowance to the inside around the neck.

9. Stuff the arms through the openings and blindstitch the edges together. Stuff the body through the neck opening. Be sure the neck is stuffed firmly, right up to the pressed edge. Do not stitch the neck opening.

Making the Head

1. Begin by making the ears. Place two Ears right sides together and stitch the seam around the contoured edge, leaving the straight edge open. Clip the curves and turn right side out.

2. Repeat step 1 to make the second ear.

3. Fold one ear in half where indicated on the pattern and baste ¼ inch from the raw edges (**Figure F**). Fold and baste the second ear in the same manner.

4. Place the Head right side up on a flat surface. Place an ear on top (**Figure G**), aligning the raw edge with the ear placement edge. The folded edge of the ear should point downward. Place the second ear on the Head, aligning it in the same manner at the ear placement markings along the opposite edge.

5. Fold the other half of the Head right side down on top of the stack, sandwiching the ears between. Stitch the contoured seam on each side of the head (**Figure G**), leaving the top of the head open between the ears. Clip the curves, turn the head

Figure H

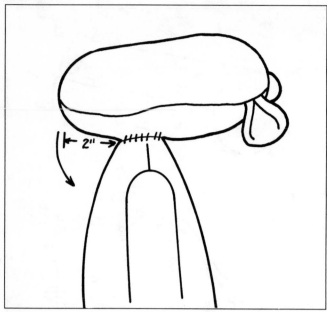

Figure I

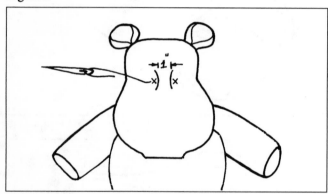

Figure J

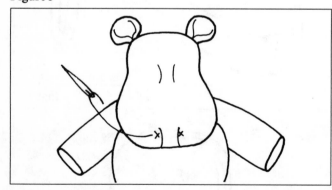

Figure K

7. To form the eye indentations, use a long sharp needle and heavy-duty gray thread. Pinch up a ridge about 1 inch wide in the center of the face (**Figure I**). Take a couple of stitches back and forth under the ridge, pull the thread to tighten the stitches, lock the stitch and cut the thread.

8. Follow the procedures in step 1 to create nostril indentations near the lower edge of the face (**Figure J**).

9. Figure K illustrates the finished face. Stitch two buttons to the face for eyes, at the indentations you sculpted in step 1. (**Note:** Buttons around small children can be hazardous if they are not securely attached. To help secure the button eyes, dab glue behind each button.) Glue an eyelash above each eye.

10. Cut two small circles from pink felt for the cheeks. Glue one cheek to each side of the face.

11. Cut two large "commas" from black felt for the nostrils. Glue the nostrils in place, as shown.

12. Cut a small heart from red felt for the mouth. Glue the mouth beneath the nostrils, as shown.

Making the Costume

1. Place the satin Front and Back Panties right sides together and stitch the crotch seam only. Press the seam open.

2. Repeat step 1, using the muslin Front and Back Panties.

3. To join the satin and muslin panty assemblies (**Figure L**), place the satin assembly right side up on a flat surface. Pin the muslin assembly right side down on top, aligning the edges. Stitch the curved leg seams. Clip the curves, turn right side out and press.

4. Fold the muslin layer in half, right sides together, so that the waist edges are even. Fold the satin layer in the same manner (**Figure M**). Begin at one side of the waist edge of the satin layer and stitch the side seam down to the leg seam; then continue to stitch the side seam until you reach the waist edge of the muslin layer. Stitch the opposite side seam in the same manner. Clip the curves and press the seams open. Tuck the muslin lining inside the satin panty.

5. Baste the muslin and satin waist edges together and encase the seam allowances in bias tape.

6. Place the satin Bodice right side up on a flat surface. Pin eyelet trim along the entire edge, placing the bound edge of the eyelet along the edge of the Bodice, with the scalloped edge to-

right side out and press the seam allowances to the inside along the opening edges. Stuff the head with fiberfill and blindstitch the opening edges.

6. Place the head over the open neck edge of the body, as shown in **Figure H**. The neck should be about 2 inches behind the chin. Carefully bend the head downward and tuck the neck edge under a bit at the front to allow for the bend. Blindstitch around the neck several times to secure the head.

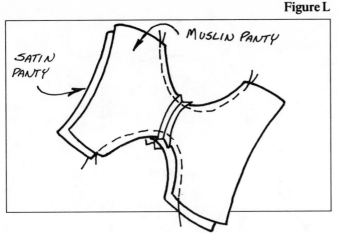

Figure L

SATIN PANTY

MUSLIN PANTY

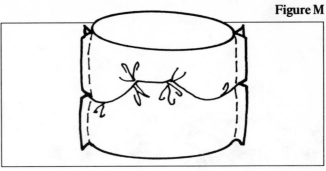

ward the center (**Figure N**). Baste the eyelet in place.

7. Pin the muslin Bodice on top and stitch the seam all the way around, leaving an opening large enough for turning. Clip the curves and corners. Turn the bodice right side out. Press the seam allowances to the inside along the opening edges and blindstitch the open edges together.

8. Tack the bodice to the front of the panty at the waist, leaving the upper and lower edges free (**Figure O**).

9. To make the tutu, stack the four net Tutu pieces, alternating colors. Baste lengthwise along the center of the stack through all four layers. Pull the thread to gather the net. Fold the net layers in half lengthwise along the gathering line and adjust the gathers to fit the panty waist. Tack the tutu around the waist edge of the panty, placing it underneath the lower point of the bodice. Fluff the net and dress Prima Hippopotarina in her costume.

10. The sequined ribbon serves as a neck strap for the bodice (**Figure P**). Tack one end of the ribbon to the back of the bodice, at the top of the heart on one side. Wrap the ribbon around her neck and tack the other end to the bodice on the other side of the heart. Cut off the excess ribbon.

Finishing

1. Place two Shoes right sides together and stitch the long contoured seam, leaving the short contoured edge open. Clip the curves and corners and turn the shoe right side out.

2. Fold in half an 18-inch length of red satin ribbon. Tack the center to the back of the shoe, as shown in **Figure Q**.

3. Repeat steps 1 and 2 to make the second shoe.

4. Slip one shoe onto a foot. Wrap the ribbons around the ankle, crossing them in the front, and tie a bow at the front of the ankle. Put the other shoe on the other foot and tie the ribbons in the same manner.

5. To make the headpiece, tightly gather the 4 x 6-inch piece of net lengthwise along the center, as you did the tutu. Tie off the gathering thread.

6. Use the remaining red and white ribbon to make streamers. Tie the ribbons in a large bow and tack the bow to the center of the gathered net, allowing the ends to hang in various lengths. Tie a small knot at the end of each ribbon streamer. Fluff the net and tack the headpiece to the top of Prima's head.

7. To adorn Prima's pudgy little wrists, cut two lengths of sequined ribbon and tack or glue one length around each wrist.

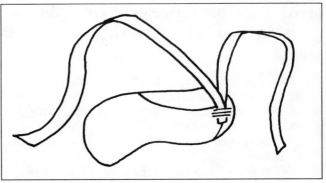

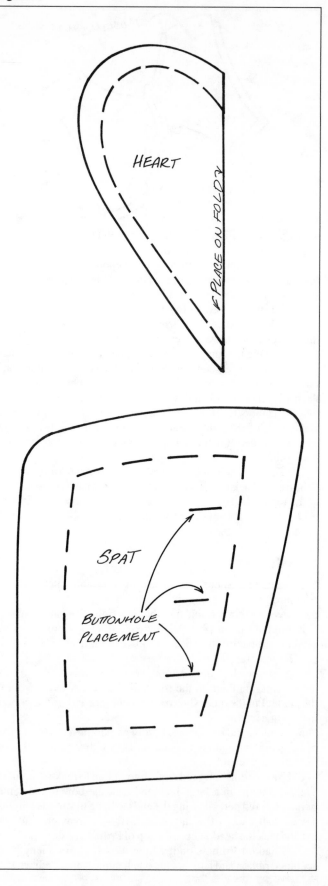

Zippity-Do-Tie

This adorable clown doesn't fool around when he teaches young ones to zip, button, snap and tie! His stuffed-fabric body is just over two feet tall and his winsome facial features are cross-stitched. Inside his zippered chest pocket beats a cross-stitched heart that says "I LUV YOU."

Materials

1⅛ yards of 44-inch striped cotton fabric for the suit and hat (We used red-and-white striped fabric.)

⅜ yard of 36-inch polka-dot cotton fabric for the vest (We used blue fabric with white dots.)

¼ yard of 44-inch thin vinyl or nylon fabric for the shoes (We used red.)

¼ yard of 44-inch satin for the hands and spats (We used white.)

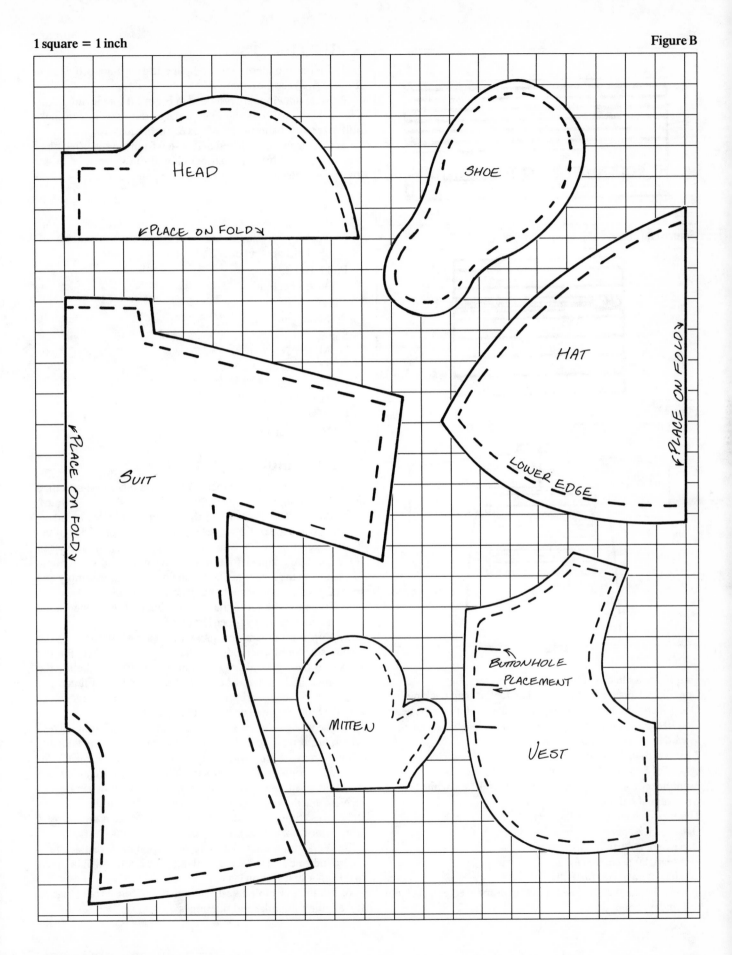

HEAD

PLACE ON FOLD

SHOE

HAT

PLACE ON FOLD

LOWER EDGE

SUIT

PLACE ON FOLD

MITTEN

BUTTONHOLE
PLACEMENT

VEST

Figure C

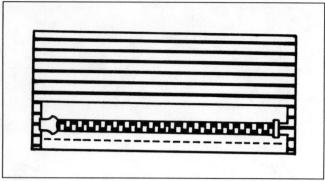

Figure D

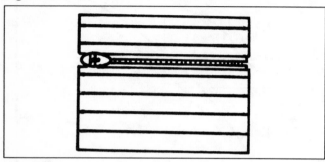

Figure E

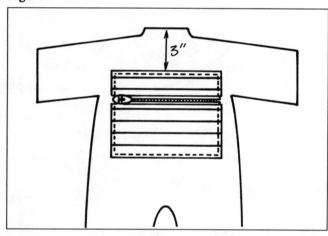

Two 10-inch squares of muslin
One 6-inch square of red cotton fabric for the heart backing
One 6-inch square of pale pink 14-count aida cloth for the heart
One 10-inch square of ivory 14-count aida cloth for the face
½ yard of ½-inch white lace trim
2 yards of 1-inch white eyelet trim
½ yard of 1-inch red grosgrain ribbon for the bow tie
Embroidery floss in charcoal, blue, red, pink and white
One skein of red rug yarn for the hair
Three ¾-inch buttons for the vest
One 5-inch zipper
One pair of colorful 27-inch shoelaces
One snap, large enough for a child to manipulate
One bag of polyester fiberfill
Sewing thread to match the fabrics; tapestry needle; 8-inch embroidery hoop

Cutting the Pieces

1. Full-size patterns for the Spat and Heart are provided in **Figure A**. Trace the patterns.

2. Scale drawings are provided in **Figure B** for the Suit, Vest, Head, Shoe, Mitten and Hat. Enlarge the drawings to make full-size paper patterns. (See Tips & Techniques.)

3. Cut the pieces as listed in this step from the specified types and colors of fabric. The stripes should run lengthwise on the two pocket pieces.

Striped:
　Suit – cut two
　Hat – cut one
　Pocket – cut one, 5 x 6½ inches
　Pocket Top – cut one, 2 x 6½ inches
Polka-Dot:
　Vest – cut four
Vinyl:
　Shoe – cut four
Satin:
　Mitten – cut four
　Spat – cut eight
Muslin:
　Head – cut two
Red:
　Heart – cut one

Suit Assembly

Note: All seams are ½ inch wide unless otherwise specified in the instructions.

1. Pin the Top Pocket and the zipper right sides together, aligning one edge of the zipper fabric with one long edge of the Top Pocket (**Figure C**). Note that the zipper is centered between the ends. Use a zipper foot on your machine and stitch about ⅛ inch from the zipper teeth, as shown. Open the assembly and press the seam allowances toward the Top Pocket.

2. Stitch the Pocket to the opposite edge of the zipper in the same manner and press open (**Figure D**).

3. Clip the corners and press the seam allowances to the wrong side along each edge of the assembled pocket. Pin the pocket to the right side of one Suit, about 3 inches below the neck edge and centered between the side edges (**Figure E**). Topstitch ¼ inch from each edge, as shown, to secure the pocket to the Suit. This will be the Suit Front.

4. The vest has no back – it consists of two lined front halves, which are sewn into the shoulder and side seams of the suit. (Zippity may be a clown, but he never will lose his vest!) Pin two Vests right sides together. Stitch the seams along the neckline, front, bottom and armhole edges, as shown in **Figure F**. Note that the shoulder and side seams are left unstitched. Clip the curves, turn right side out and press. Make a second vest front in the same manner, using the two remaining Vests.

5. Work three buttonholes in one assembled vest section, where indicated on the scale drawing. The buttons will be sewn to the other vest section later.

6. Pin the assembled vest sections to the Suit Front (**Figure G**), aligning shoulder and side edges.

Figure F

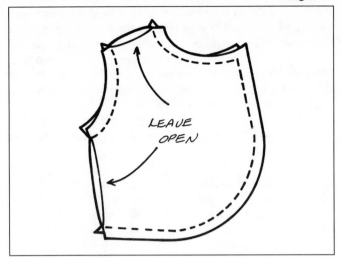

Figure G

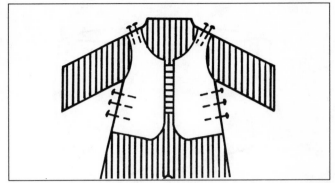

Figure H

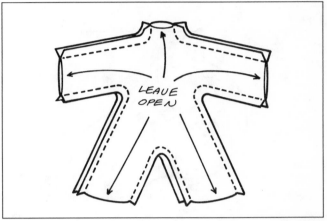

Figure I

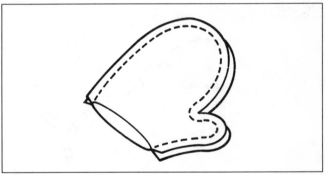

Figure J

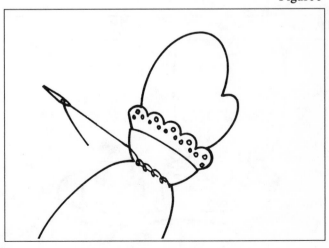

7. Pin the Suit Back to the Suit Front, with right sides together. (The vests will be sandwiched between the two Suits.) Stitch the seams, as shown in **Figure H**, leaving the neck edge and the arm and leg ends open. Clip the curves and corners, turn right side out and press.

8. Press the seam allowances to the inside around the neck, arm and leg openings of the assembled suit. Measure around one arm opening and cut a length of eyelet trim slightly longer. Topstitch the trim to the pressed arm edge, folding under the raw ends. Topstitch eyelet trim to the other arm and both leg openings in the same manner.

9. Baste around each arm 1 inch from the open end. Do not cut off the tails of thread, as they will later be pulled to gather the arm around a mitten. In the same manner, baste 1 inch from the open end of each leg.

10. Stuff the suit with fiberfill – not so tightly that the arms and legs will not bend but enough to give Zippity support. Do not stuff below the basting thread at the end of each arm and leg and leave about ½ inch unstuffed at the neck edge.

11. Bring the two vest halves together across the front of the suit and mark the button placement. Sew on the three buttons very securely, so your child will not be able to pull them off.

Mittens and Shoes

1. Pin two Mittens right sides together. Stitch the seam all the way along the contoured edge (**Figure I**), leaving the wrist edge open. Clip the curves and corners and turn right side out. Stuff with fiberfill right up to the open end and baste the open edges together. Make a second mitten in the same manner.

2. Insert the open end of a mitten inside one of Zippity's arms, with the thumb pointing upward. Pull the basting thread to gather the arm tightly around the mitten and tie off. Whipstitch around the wrist two or three times, over the basting stitches, to secure the mitten to the suit fabric (**Figure J**). Attach the second mitten to the other arm in the same manner.

3. Pin half of the snap to each mitten, on the palm side near the fingertip end. Bring the arms across the front of the suit and snap the mittens together to test the snap placement. Sew the snaps in place.

Figure K

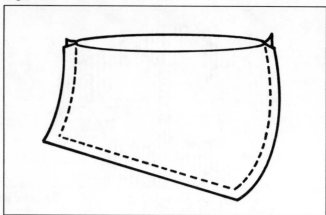

Figure L

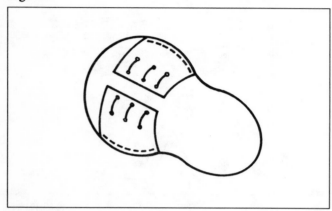

Figure M

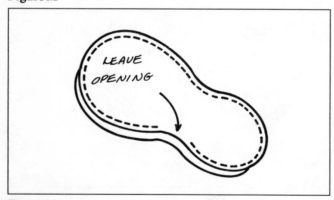

LEAVE OPENING

Figure N

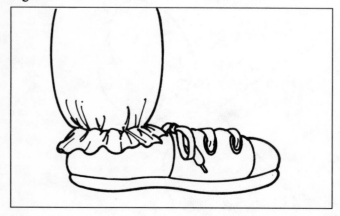

4. The feet will look like big clown sneakers with white spats. Pin two Spats right sides together. Stitch the seams along both ends and the buttonhole edge (**Figure K**), leaving the opposite edge unstitched. Clip the curves and corners, turn right side out and press. Baste the open edges together inside the seam line. Work three buttonholes where indicated on the pattern. Repeat this step three more times, using the six remaining Spats, so that you have four assembled spats.

5. Place two assembled spats on the right side of one vinyl Shoe, as shown in **Figure L**. Baste the spats to the Shoe over the existing basting stitches.

6. Pin a second Shoe right side down on top of the spats and first Shoe. Stitch the seam around the edge, as shown in **Figure M**, leaving a 2- or 3-inch opening along one side. Clip the curves, turn right side out and press the seam allowances to the inside along the opening. Stuff the shoe and blindstitch the opening edges together.

7. Bring the two spats together on top of the shoe. Thread a shoelace through the buttonholes, starting at the toe end and working toward the heel. Tie the lace in a large bow.

8. Repeat steps 5, 6 and 7 to assemble a second shoe.

9. Pull the basting thread to gather the lower end of one leg, so that the opening is about 1¼ inches in diameter. Place the leg on top of an assembled shoe (**Figure N**). Make sure that the toe end of the shoe faces the same direction as the front of the suit. Whipstitch over the gathering line two or three times to secure the leg fabric to the shoe. Repeat this step to attach the second shoe to the other leg.

Making the Head

1. If you have never done counted cross-stitch before, please refer to Tips & Techniques. A stitching graph for Zippity's face is provided in **Figure O**. Center the full-size Head pattern on the ivory-colored aida cloth square and trace the outline of the pattern onto the cloth. Before you begin stitching, count spaces to determine where to begin, so the features will be placed correctly within the pattern outline. We worked the eye outlines in charcoal, the irises in blue, the small eye and nose highlights in white, the nose and outer mouth outline in red, the lip line in charcoal and the heart-shaped cheek spots in pink.

2. Trim the aida cloth along the traced pattern outline. Place the aida Head right side up on top of one of the muslin Heads and baste the layers together close to the edges. Now pin the two muslin Heads right sides together, so that the aida layer is sandwiched between. Stitch the seam along the contoured edge, leaving the straight neck edge open. Clip the curves, turn right side out and press gently.

3. Stuff the head firmly, smoothing out the wrinkles along the curved seam. Baste the open neck edges together.

4. Insert the neck edge of the assembled head into the neck opening of the stuffed suit. Whipstitch around the neck several times to secure the assembly. Glue or blindstitch a length of eyelet trim around the neck seam, with the scalloped edge pointing upward. Tie the red grosgrain ribbon into a bow and tack it to the suit front just below the eyelet.

5. A hat and hair will save poor Zippity from his present baldness. Fold the Hat in half along the "place on fold" line, with

Fredd Redd
page 21

Big Hoppy
page 30

Prima Hippopotarina
page 38

Miss Lucie
page 51

Sleepy Sally
page 51

Murphy
page 61

Spoon Dolls
page 67

The Old Lady in the Shoe
page 73

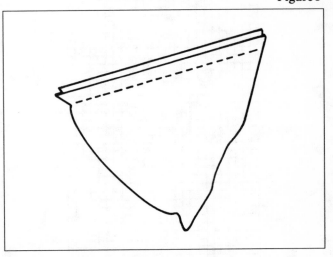

right sides together. Stitch the side seam along the edge designated on the pattern, leaving the lower edge open (**Figure P**). Clip the curve and corners, turn right side out and press. Press the hem allowance to the wrong side of the fabric around the lower edge.

6. Stuff the hat lightly and place it on Zippity's head, a little off center and at an angle. Blindstitch the hat in place around the pressed lower edge. Fold the point over to one side and tack it to the hat.

7. To make a pompom for the hat, cut about forty 2-inch lengths of rug yarn. Tie them together at the center, using another short yarn length. Now fold the yarn ends all in the same direction (**Figure Q**) and tie again just above the center tie. Fluff the ends to form a sphere. Tack the pompom to the tip of Zippity's hat.

8. To make Zippity's curly hair, use a continuous length of

Figure Q

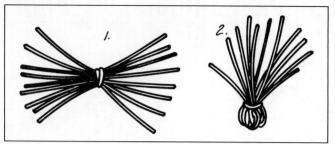

Figure R

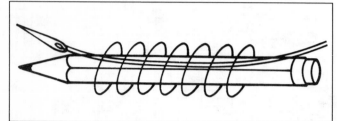

Figure S

BACK OF HEAD

Figure T

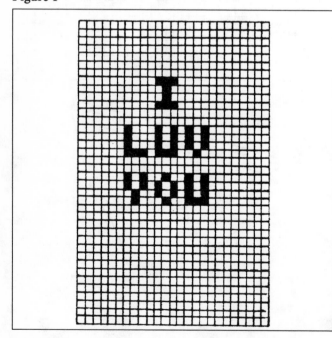

Figure U

I LUV YOU

3/8"

rug yarn and a needle and matching thread. Tack one end of the yarn to his head, just below the hat and in front of the head seam. Wrap the yarn loosely around a pencil (or anything else of similar shape – it can be fatter) about twenty times. Insert the needle and thread between the yarn loops and the pencil (**Figure R**), compressing the loops, and pull the needle out the other end. Remove the pencil and tack the curl to Zippity's head where the original yarn end was attached.

9. Continue working in this manner, tacking closely spaced curls along the back hairline and up to the hat on the opposite side of the face (**Figure S**). When the last curl is completed, tack the yarn end to the head securely.

10. To finish the hair, make two large yarn pompoms as you did for the hat, only bigger. Stitch one to each side of the face, just below the hat, at the top of the hairline.

You Gotta Have Heart…

1. Place the full-size Heart pattern on top of the pink aida cloth and trace the outline. A stitching graph for the "I LUV YOU" motto is provided in **Figure T**. Work the motto in the center of the heart outline, using red floss.

2. Cut the aida cloth along the traced heart outline. Staystitch close to the edge to keep the cloth from fraying.

3. Pin lace trim to the right side of the aida Heart, ⅜ inch from the edge, as shown in **Figure U**. Baste the lace in place just inside the outer edge.

4. Pin the red-fabric Heart to the aida Heart, with right sides together. (The lace will be sandwiched between.) Stitch the seam along the edge, leaving a 2-inch opening. Clip the curves and corners, turn right side out and press gently. Press the seam allowances to the inside along the opening.

5. Stuff the heart firmly. Blindstitch the opening edges.

6. Place the heart in Zippity's pocket, and he's ready to teach!

Miss Lucie & Sleepy Sally

These 3-foot-tall dolls are just perfect for big hugs. Their bodies are stuffed fabric and they have soft-sculpted facial features. Instructions are included for Lucie's dress and bloomers, or she can wear clothes your little ones have outgrown. Sally wears a purchased toddler's size 4 sleeper.

Materials

For Lucie:

1½ yards of calico fabric for the dress
½ yard of white batiste fabric for the bloomers
1 yard of ¼-inch satin ribbon that coordinates with the calico
16-inch length of ¾-inch gathered white lace trim
1½ yards of wide satin ribbon
½ yard of ½-inch elastic

1 yard of ¼-inch elastic
Small amounts of felt in black, white and blue

For Sally:

A toddler's size 4 sleeper
1 yard of ¾-inch satin ribbon in a color that coordinates with the sleeper
Small amount of red embroidery floss
Small amounts of felt in black and pink

For *each* doll:

2 yards of medium-weight flesh-tone stretchy knit fabric for the body and head
2½ pounds of polyester fiberfill
Three skeins of rug yarn for the hair (We used brown for Lucie and yellow for Sally.)
Hot-melt glue and a glue gun (or white glue)
Long sharp needle; heavy-duty thread in flesh-tone and a color to match the rug yarn; and regular thread to match the fabrics
Cosmetic cheek blusher

For the teddy bear:

14 x 28-inch piece of calico fabric
Embroidery floss for the facial features (We used black.)
¾- or 1-inch-diameter pompom for the nose (We used black.)
Small amount of pink felt for the cheek spots
22-inch length of ¾-inch satin ribbon for the bow tie
Thread to match the calico
Small amount of polyester fiberfill

Figure A

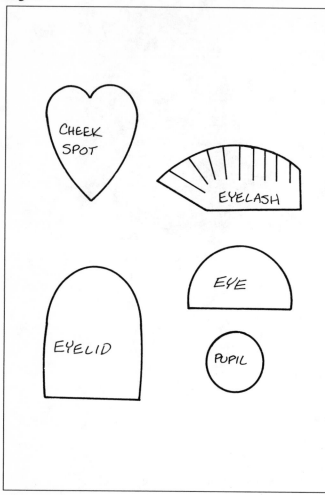

Cutting the Pieces

1. Full-size patterns are provided in **Figure A** for the Eyelash, Eye, Pupil, Eyelid and Cheek Spot. Trace the patterns onto tracing paper or dressmaker's paper.

2. Scale drawings are provided in **Figures B** and **C** for the Dress Back, Dress Front, Sleeve, Bloomers, Head, Face, Head Back, Arm, Torso, Foot, Sole, Teddy Bear and Leg. (Notations on the drawings indicate which pieces belong to which doll.) Enlarge the drawings to make full-size paper patterns. (See Tips & Techniques.)

3. Cut from flesh-tone knit fabric the following pieces for *each* doll:

   Head – cut two
   Head Back – cut one
   Face – cut one
   Nose – cut one, 2½-inch-diameter circle
   Torso – cut two
   Arm – cut four
   Leg – cut four
   Foot – cut four
   Sole – cut two
   Eyelid (for Sally only) – cut two

4. Cut the following felt pieces:

Cheek Spot (Sally) – cut two pink
Eyelash – cut four black
Pupil (Lucie) – cut two blue

5. Cut from calico the following pieces for Lucie's clothing:
   Dress Front – cut one
   Dress Back – cut two
   Sleeve – cut two

6. Cut from white batiste two Bloomers for Lucie.

7. Cut two Teddy Bears from calico.

MISS LUCIE

Making the Body

1. Pin the two Torsos right sides together and stitch the seams, as shown in **Figure D**. Leave neck and arm openings where indicated and leave the lower edge open. Clip the corners and curves and press the seams open.

2. Pin two Arms right sides together and stitch the seam, leaving the shoulder end open. Clip the curves and press the seams open. Turn the arm right side out and stuff. Make a second arm in same manner.

3. To soft-sculpt the fingers, use a long sharp needle and flesh-tone heavy-duty thread. Follow the entry and exit points illustrated in **Figure E**.

   a. Insert the needle on the palm side of the hand at point 1. This will be the base of the first finger. Push the needle through the hand and exit at point 1 on the back.

   b. Wrap the thread around the end of the hand. Enter on the palm side at point 1 and exit on the back at point 1. Pull the thread to form one finger. Lock the stitch.

   c. Reenter at 1, take a small stitch underneath the surface and exit at the base of the second finger, point 2.

   d. Repeat sub-steps a through c two more times at points 2 and 3 to form the remaining fingers.

4. Pin two Legs right sides together and stitch the seams, leaving both ends open. Clip the corners, press the seams open and turn right side out. Make a second leg in the same manner.

5. Pin two Foot pieces right sides together. Stitch the seams, leaving leg and sole openings, as shown in **Figure F**. Clip the curves and press. Make a second foot in the same manner and leave the feet turned inside out.

6. Slip a foot over the lower end of one leg (**Figure G**), placing right sides together and aligning the ankle edges. Stitch the ankle seam and press it open. Turn the foot downward, so it is right side out.

7. Turn the entire leg-and-foot assembly wrong side out. Baste the Sole to the open edge of the foot (**Figure H**), placing right sides together. Stitch the seam, clip the curves and press. Turn the assembly right side out and stuff the foot and leg.

8. Finish the remaining leg and foot in the same manner.

9. The torso should still be wrong side out. Slip an arm into each arm opening, with thumbs pointing upward. (The arms should be sandwiched between the two torso layers.) Pin the arms into the arm openings and stitch in place (**Figure I**). Turn the torso right side out and stuff gently, leaving ½ inch unstuffed at the lower edge.

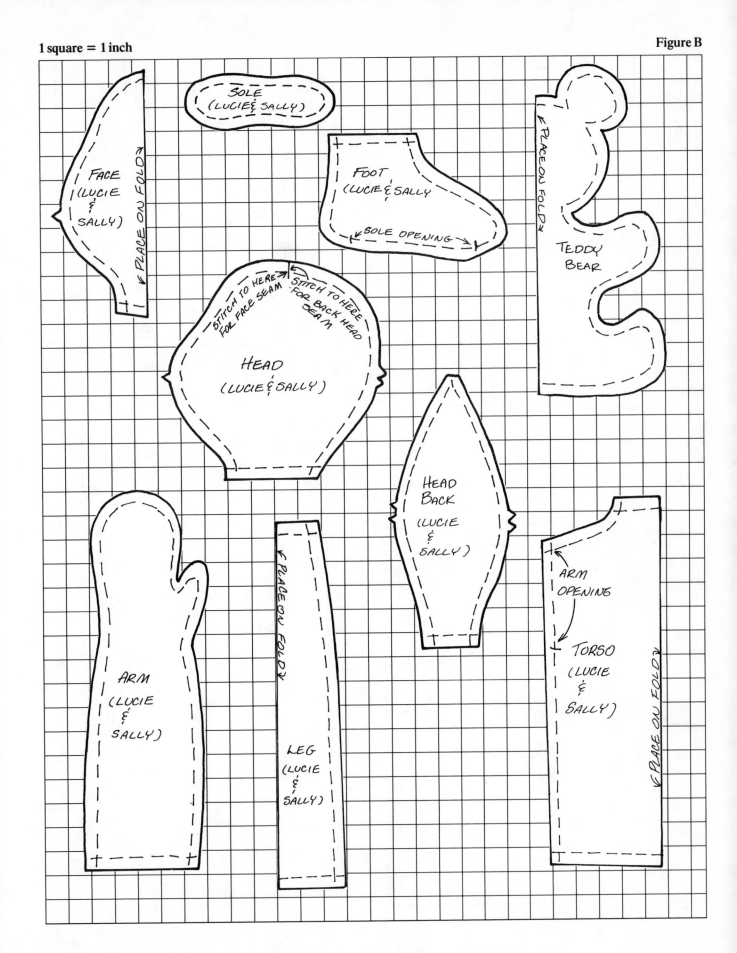

SOLE
(LUCIE & SALLY)

FACE
(LUCIE & SALLY)

← PLACE ON FOLD →

FOOT
(LUCIE & SALLY)

← SOLE OPENING →

← PLACE ON FOLD →

TEDDY BEAR

STITCH TO HERE FOR FACE SEAM

STITCH TO HERE FOR BACK HEAD SEAM

HEAD
(LUCIE & SALLY)

HEAD BACK
(LUCIE & SALLY)

ARM OPENING

TORSO
(LUCIE & SALLY)

← PLACE ON FOLD →

ARM
(LUCIE & SALLY)

← PLACE ON FOLD →

LEG
(LUCIE & SALLY)

Figure C

1 square = 1 inch

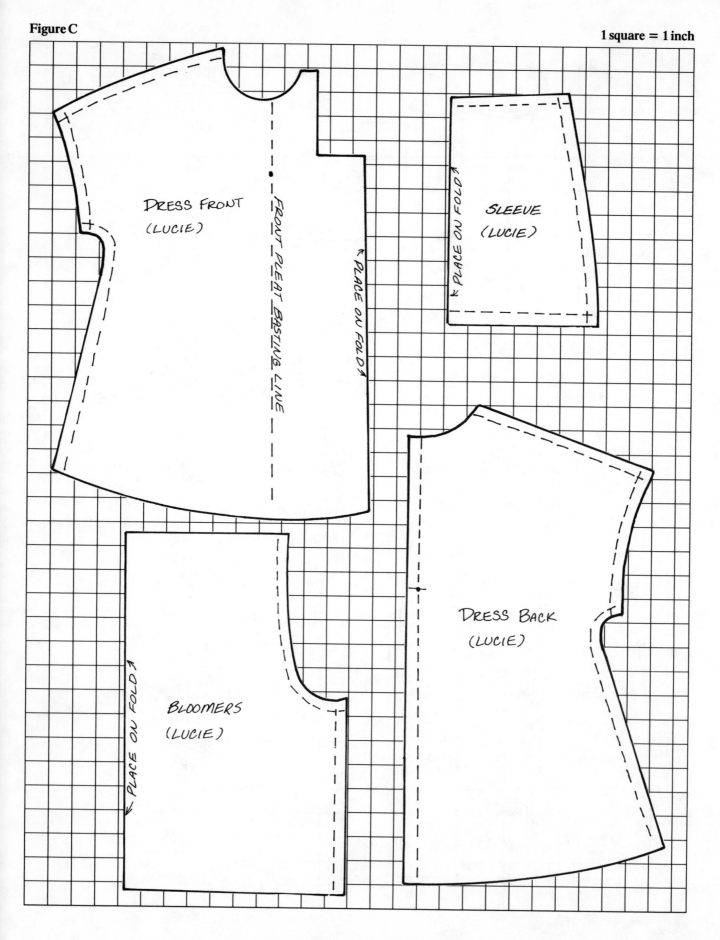

DRESS FRONT
(LUCIE)

FRONT PLEAT BASTING LINE

←PLACE ON FOLD→

SLEEVE
(LUCIE)

←PLACE ON FOLD→

DRESS BACK
(LUCIE)

BLOOMERS
(LUCIE)

←PLACE ON FOLD→

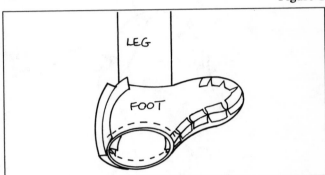

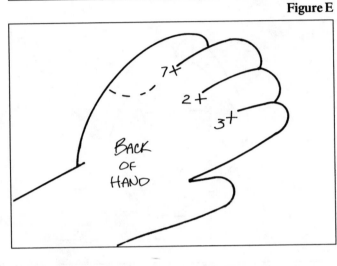

10. Pin the tops of the legs to the lower edge of the front torso, with toes pointing toward the body (**Figure J**). Stitch ¼ inch from the edge to attach the legs to the front torso only.

11. Turn the legs downward and press the seam allowance to the inside around the remainder of the lower torso edge. Whipstitch together the pressed front and back lower edges, securing the legs at the same time.

Making the Head

1. Place one Head right side up on a flat surface. Pin the Face right side down on top, matching notches, as shown in **Figure K**. Stitch the seam, easing the curves. Clip the curves and press the seam open.

2. Place the second Head right side up on a flat surface. Pin the head-and-face assembly right side down on top, matching notches, as shown in **Figure L**. Stitch the seam, easing the curves. Clip the curves and press the seam open.

3. Place the head-and-face assembly right side up on a flat surface. Pin the Head Back right side down on top, matching notches along one edge, as shown in **Figure M**. Stitch the seam, easing the curves. Clip the curves and press the seam open.

4. Pin the free edge of the Head Back to the free edge of the head assembly, with right sides together. Stitch the seam, leaving the neck edge open (**Figure N**). Clip the curves and press the seam open. Turn the head right side out and stuff firmly with polyester fiberfill.

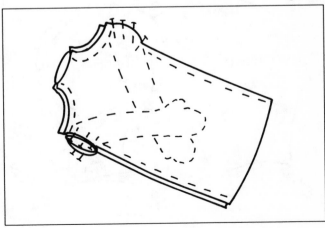

Figure I

Figure J

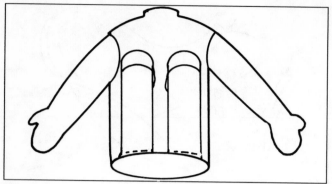

Figure K

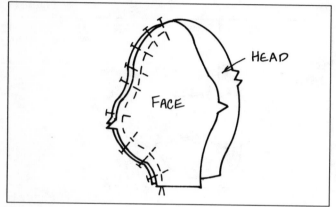

Figure L

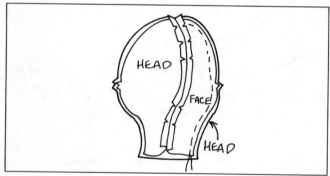

Figure M

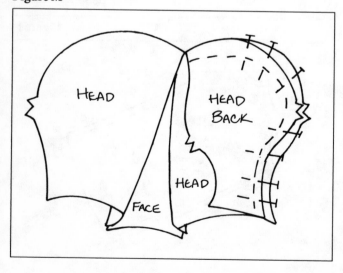

Figure N

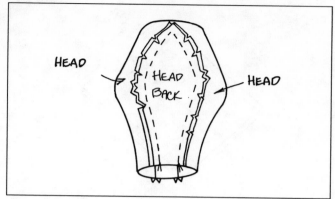

Figure O

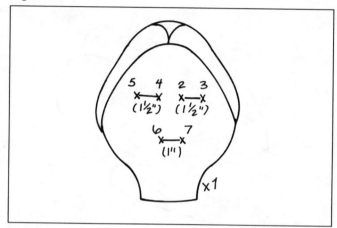

Figure P

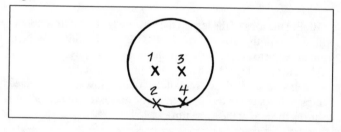

5. To soft-sculpt the facial features, use a long sharp needle and flesh-tone heavy-duty thread. Follow the entry and exit points illustrated in **Figure O.**

   a. To make the eye lines, enter at point 1, push the needle through the head and exit at point 2.

   b. Pull the thread across the surface about 1½ inches, enter at 3 and exit at 4.

   c. Pull the thread across the surface, enter at 5 and exit at 4. Gently pull the thread until the eyes appear. Lock the stitch at 4 and cut the thread.

   d. To form the mouth, enter at 1 and exit at 6.

   e. Pull the thread across the surface about 1 inch, enter at 7 and exit at 6. Pull the thread until the mouth forms, lock the stitch at 6 and cut the thread.

6. To make the nose, baste around the edge of the Nose piece. Place a small wad of fiberfill inside the nose and pull the basting threads to gather the fabric. Tie off the gathering thread. Refer to **Figure P** as you sculpt the nostrils.

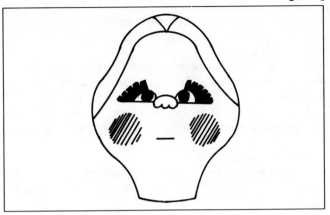

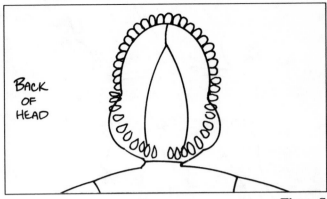

BACK
OF
HEAD

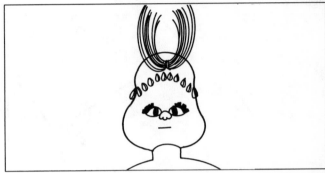

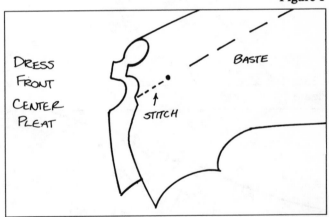

DRESS
FRONT
CENTER
PLEAT

BASTE

STITCH

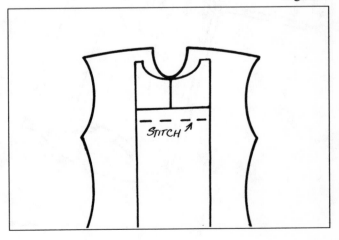

STITCH

a. Enter from the underside of the nose and exit at 1.

b. Pull the thread across the surface and enter at 2. Push the needle through the nose and exit at 3.

c. Pull the thread across the surface and enter at 4. Lock the stitch at 4, pulling the thread to form the nostrils.

7. Glue and blindstitch the nose to Lucie's face just below and between the soft-sculpted eye lines.

8. Glue the felt Eyes, Eyelashes and Pupils to the face, as shown in **Figure Q**. Use cosmetic cheek blusher to add color to Lucie's cheeks, nose and mouth.

9. Press the seam allowance to the inside of the torso around the open neck edge. Insert the neck edge of the head and whipstitch securely in place.

10. To make the hair, you'll be working with a continuous length of yarn, heavy-duty thread in a coordinating color and a long sharp needle. Stitch one end of the yarn to the back of the head at the base. Form a 2-inch loop of yarn and stitch it to the head. Continue working around the hairline, forming loops and stitching them in place until you reach the starting point again (**Figure R**).

11. Cut the remaining yarn into 2½-foot lengths and divide it into separate bunches, each containing eight or nine strands. Fold one bunch in half and stitch it to the head at the base of one loop near the front of the head, as shown in **Figure S**. Follow the same procedure to stitch bunches of yarn all the way around the line of loops.

12. Use a pencil to draw a line down the center of Lucie's head. Stitch bunches of yarn to the head on each side of the center line.

13. To make one ponytail, gather all the yarn on one side of the head and pull it together. Tie a piece of yarn around the ponytail. Cut the wide ribbon into two equal lengths and tie one around the ponytail over the yarn, forming a bow. Make a second ponytail in the same manner.

Making the Dress

1. Fold the Dress Front right sides together and stitch the center pleat from the neckline to the small circle (**Figure T**). Baste the pleat from the small circle to the lower edge.

2. Open the Dress Front and press the pleat, dividing it equally on either side of the stitching. Stitch across the top of the pressed pleat, as shown in **Figure U**. Remove the basting.

Figure V

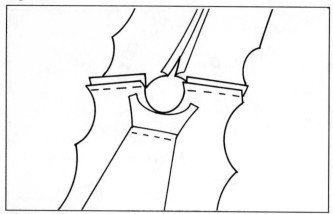

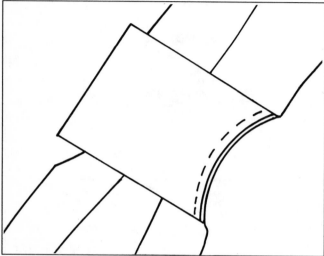

Figure X

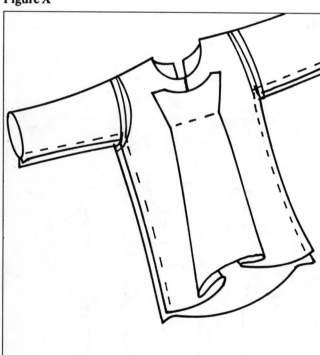

3. Pin the two Dress Backs right sides together and stitch the center back seam from the lower edge to the small circle. Leave the upper 6 inches open. Press the seam open. Press the seam allowances to the wrong side of the fabric along the unstitched portion of the seam.

4. Pin the front and back dress assemblies right sides together along the shoulder seams. Stitch the seams, as shown in **Figure V**, and press open.

5. Pin one Sleeve to the dress along one armhole edge, placing right sides together. Stitch the seam (**Figure W**) and press both seam allowances toward the dress. Attach the second Sleeve in the same manner.

6. Stitch a 7-inch length of ¼-inch elastic to the wrong side of each sleeve 2½ inches from the lower edge, stretching the elastic as you stitch.

7. Fold the dress right sides together and stitch the underarm and side seam on each side (**Figure X**). Press the seams open.

8. Press and stitch a ½-inch hem to the wrong side of each sleeve around the lower edge.

9. Press a ¼-inch hem to the wrong side of the dress around the neck edge. Stitch the ¾-inch lace trim around the neckline.

10. Cut the narrower satin ribbon into two equal lengths and stitch one to each upper corner of the dress back opening. The ribbon ties will be used to hold the dress together.

11. Hem the lower edge of the dress to the desired length.

Making the Bloomers

1. Pin the two Bloomers right sides together and stitch the center front and back seams, as shown in **Figure Y**.

2. Refold the bloomers, still right sides together, matching the center front and back seams. Stitch the inner leg seam, as shown in **Figure Z**.

3. Press a ¼-inch allowance to the wrong side of the fabric around the waist edge. To form a casing for the elastic, fold the same edge over again about ¾ inch. Stitch close to the pressed edge, leaving a short opening. Cut a length of elastic 2 inches shorter than Lucie's waist measurement and thread it through the casing. Stitch together the ends of the elastic and tuck them inside the casing. Whipstitch the opening.

4. Stitch a length of elastic to the wrong side of each bloomer leg about 2½ inches from the lower edge, as you did for the dress sleeves. Stitch a narrow hem around the lower edge of each leg, as you did for the dress sleeves.

SLEEPY SALLY

Making the Head and Body

The body and head assemblies for Sally are identical to those for Lucie. Follow the instructions for Lucie under the headings "Making the Body" and "Making the Head," but do not follow Lucie's instructions for facial features or hair. Dress Sleepy Sally in her sleeper.

Facial Features and Hair

1. Sally's facial features are shown in **Figure AA**. Form and soft-sculpt Sally's nose in the same manner as you did Lucie's.

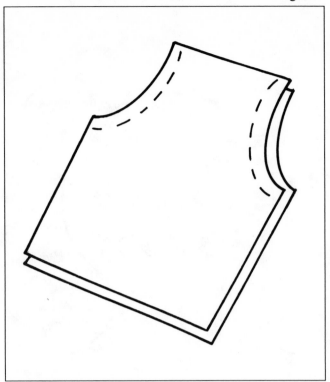

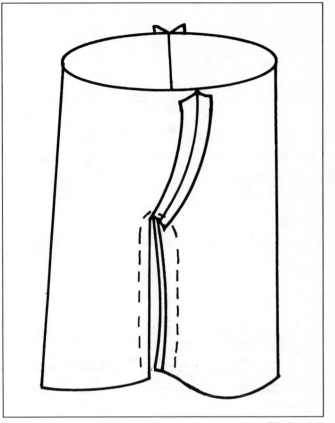

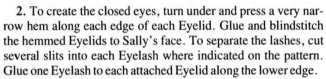

Figure AA

2. To create the closed eyes, turn under and press a very narrow hem along each edge of each Eyelid. Glue and blindstitch the hemmed Eyelids to Sally's face. To separate the lashes, cut several slits into each Eyelash where indicated on the pattern. Glue one Eyelash to each attached Eyelid along the lower edge.

3. To create Sally's mouth, use red embroidery floss to work a slightly curved line of split stitches, back stitches or chain stitches where indicated in **Figure AA**. (See Tips & Techniques on embroidery.)

4. Glue a heart-shaped Cheek Spot to each cheek. You may wish to blindstitch around them. Use a little cosmetic blusher across Sally's cheeks and nose.

5. Sally's yarn hair is braided on each side and includes a cute little topknot for bangs (**Figure BB**). Cut four 6-inch lengths of yarn for the braid ties and put them aside for the moment. Cut all of the remaining yarn into 30-inch strands. Put three strands aside to be used later for the bangs.

6. Place several yarn strands across her head and stitch along the center part to attach. You can include more than one strand in each stitch, but be sure to pull the thread fairly tight with each stitch. Use all of the yarn, working all the way down to neck level at the back of the head. It's not a bad idea to run a bead of glue along the part after the stitching is completed.

7. Spread a little glue on Sally's head on each side of the center part and smooth the yarn down over the head to about cheek level on each side. On one side of the head, gather the yarn at cheek level, wrap one of the 6-inch yarn lengths around the hair and tie off. (Do not wrap too tightly.) Separate the hair into three sections below the tie and make a braid. Use a second 6-inch yarn length to tie off the braid near the bottom. Repeat these procedures to braid the hair on the opposite side of the head.

Figure BB

Figure CC

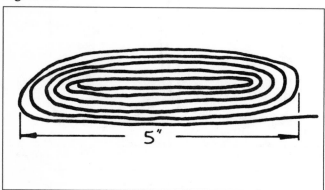

Figure DD

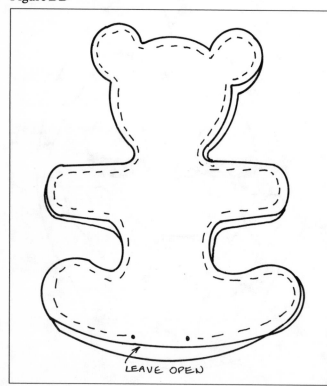

LEAVE OPEN

Figure EE

8. Cut the 1-yard length of satin ribbon in half and cut both ends of each piece at an angle. Use one of them to tie off each braid near the bottom, wrapping it over the small yarn tie. Tie the ribbon in a bow.

9. To create the bangs, wrap the remaining three lengths of yarn into a continuous loop about 5 inches long, as shown in **Figure CC**. Gather the loop at the center and wrap it tightly, using a free end of the yarn. Tie off the center wrapping and stitch the topknot to Sally's head at the front of the center part. Fluff the bangs.

Making the Teddy Bear

1. Pin the two Teddy Bears right sides together. Stitch a continuous seam all the way around, leaving an opening at the bottom for stuffing (**Figure DD**). Clip the curves and corners and turn the body right side out. Press the seam allowances to the inside along the opening.

2. Stuff the body firmly with fiberfill, but you need not stuff the ears. Whipstitch the opening edges together.

3. The teddy bear's face is shown in **Figure EE**. Thread an embroidery needle with all six strands of floss. To create each eye, work four straight stitches in an asterisk pattern, as shown. To create the mouth lines, work long straight stitches below the eyes, as shown. Tie off the floss securely.

4. Cut a small circle of pink felt for each cheek spot. Glue them to the face, as shown, placing them over the ends of the stitched mouth lines. Glue and stitch the pompom to the face over the upper end of the stitched nose-mouth line.

5. Cut the ends of the ribbon at an angle. Wrap the ribbon around the bear's neck and tie in a bow at the front.

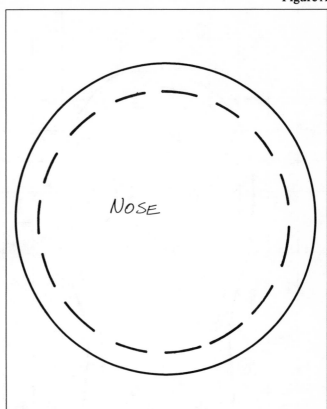

Murphy

Five feet tall and full of fun! Murphy is a dancing doll that loves to trip the light fantastic. Thanks to elastic straps across his feet he can perform the new dance steps along with a partner. Murphy may be tall, but he weighs only about 5 pounds.

Materials

2¼ yards of 45-inch white medium-weight poly-cotton knit fabric for the body
4 yards of 45-inch striped fabric for the suit
4-inch-square piece of red fabric for the nose
One skein of bright-colored rug yarn for Murphy's hair
½ yard of 30-inch black vinyl or fabric for the shoes
7 x 48-inch piece of felt to match the striped fabric for the collar
½ yard of 1-inch eyelet trim
1 yard of ¼-inch elastic
14-inch length of ½-inch elastic for the collar
One package of white extra-wide bias tape
3-inch length of nylon fastener strip
Five bags of polyester fiberfill
Long sharp needle; heavy-duty white thread; and regular thread to match the fabrics
Acrylic paints (black and deep red); and fine-tipped artist's brush (or felt-tip markers)

Cutting the Pieces

1. A full-size pattern for the Nose is provided in **Figure A**. Trace the pattern.
2. Scale drawings are provided in **Figure B** for Murphy's Shoe, Head, Ear and Hand. Enlarge the drawings to make full-size paper patterns. (See Tips & Techniques.)
3. Cut the pieces as listed in this step from the specified types and colors of fabric.

White poly-cotton:
    Head – cut one
    Hand – cut four
    Ear – cut four
    Body – cut two, 18 x 24 inches
    Arm – cut two, 13 x 20 inches
    Leg – cut two, 14 x 21 inches
Striped fabric:
    Sleeve – cut four, 16 x 24 inches
    Suit – cut two, 42 x 52 inches
Red:
    Nose – cut one
Black:
    Shoe – cut four

Making the Head

Note: All seams are ½ inch unless otherwise specified.

1. Fold the Head in half, placing right sides together. Stitch the seam around the contoured edge, leaving the neck edge open

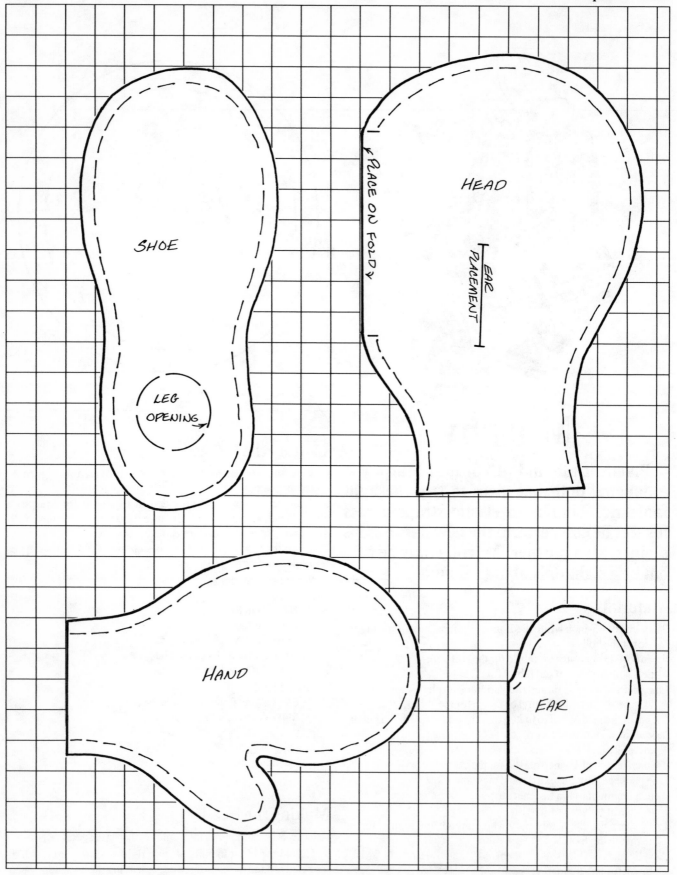

SHOE

LEG OPENING

PLACE ON FOLD

HEAD

EAR PLACEMENT

HAND

EAR

Figure C   **Figure D**

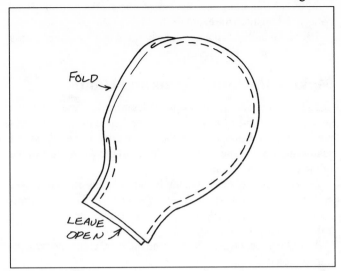

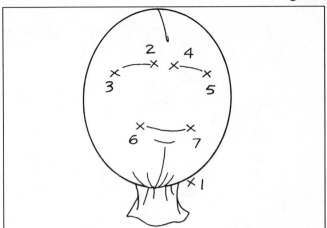

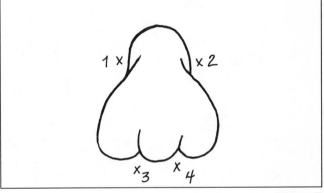

(**Figure C**). Clip the curve, turn right side out and press the seam allowances to the inside along the opening.

2. Lightly stuff the head and neck, using approximately one bag of fiberfill. Smooth out the wrinkles along the curves.

3. To soft-sculpt the eyes and mouth, use heavy-duty thread and a long sharp needle and follow the entry and exit points illustrated in **Figure D**.

    a. To make the eyes, enter at 1 and exit at 2. Reenter at 2 and exit at 3.

    b. Pull the thread across the surface, enter at 2 and exit at point 4.

    c. Pull the thread across the surface, enter at 5 and exit at 4. Gently pull the thread until the eyes appear and lock the stitch at 4.

    d. To form the mouth, reenter at 4 and exit at 6.

    e. Pull the thread across the surface, enter at 7 and exit at 6. Gently pull the thread until a smile forms. Lock the stitch and cut the thread.

4. To make the nose, baste along the seam line of the Nose piece. Place a small ball of fiberfill in the center of the nose on the wrong side of the fabric. Pull the basting threads to gather the edge around the fiberfill. Tie off the gathers.

5. To soft-sculpt the nostrils, use heavy-duty thread and a long sharp needle. Follow the entry and exit points illustrated in **Figure E**.

    a. Enter at 1 and exit at 3.

    b. Enter ¼ inch directly above 3 and exit at 2.

    c. Reenter at 2 and exit at 4.

    d. Enter ¼ inch directly above 4 and exit at 1. Lock the stitch under the bridge of the nose.

6. Whipstitch the finished nose to Murphy's face, placing the gathered side against the face.

7. To finish the face, paint or draw the eyelids, rosy cheeks, laugh lines and lower lips, as shown in **Figure F**.

8. Place two Ears right sides together and stitch the seam along the contoured edge, leaving the straight edge open. Clip the curves, turn right side out and press the seam allowances to the inside along the opening.

9. Stuff the ear lightly with fiberfill. Place it against

Figure G

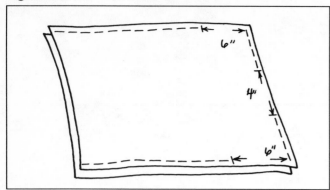

Figure H

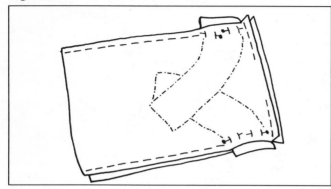

Figure I

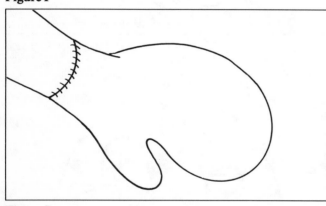

Figure J

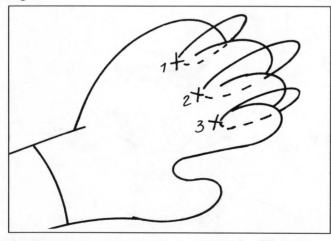

Murphy's head along the placement line marked on the Head pattern. Blindstitch the ear to the head.

10. Make and attach a second ear in the same manner, using the two remaining Ear pieces.

Making the Body, Arms and Hands

1. Place the two Bodies right sides together and stitch the seams, as shown in **Figure G**, leaving 4- and 6-inch openings where indicated and leaving the lower edge open. Press the seams open. Press the seam allowances to the wrong side of the fabric along each opening.

2. Fold one Arm in half lengthwise, placing right sides together and stitch the seam along the long edge. Leave the ends open. Press the seam allowances to the wrong side of the fabric around the lower open end.

3. Make a second arm in the same manner, using the remaining Arm piece.

4. Place two Hands right sides together. Stitch the seam along the long contoured edge, leaving the wrist open. Clip the curves and turn right side out. Press the seam allowances to the inside along the opening edges and stuff lightly with fiberfill.

5. Make another hand in the same manner, using the remaining two Hand pieces.

6. Turn each arm right side out and turn the body inside out. Slip one arm into each arm opening of the body so that the arms are sandwiched between the two layers of the body. Pin them in place at the arm openings (**Figure H**). Whipstitch the seams, using heavy-duty thread. Turn the body right side out.

7. Insert the wrist end of one hand inside the lower opening of one arm (**Figure I**). Turn the arm seam allowance to the inside and whipstitch around the edge. Glue or sew eyelet trim over the whipstitched seam. Attach the other hand. Stuff each arm lightly with fiberfill, working from inside the body.

8. Slip the head into the neck opening of the body and whipstitch securely in place.

9. To soft-sculpt the fingers, use heavy-duty thread and a long sharp needle and follow the entry and exit points illustrated in **Figure J**.

    a. To form the base of the first finger, enter at point 1 on the palm and exit directly opposite 1 on the back.

    b. Wrap the thread around the end of the hand, reenter at 1 on the palm and exit at 1 on the back.

    c. Pull the thread to form the first finger and lock the stitch at point 1.

    d. To form the base of the second finger, reenter at 1, push the needle under the surface and exit at 2 on the back of the hand.

    e. Repeat steps b through d at points 2 and 3 to form the remaining fingers. When you have completed the steps at point 3, lock the stitch and cut the thread.

10. To create Murphy's hair, place the skein of yarn across the center of his head, as shown in **Figure K**. Stitch the yarn to his head along the center part, using heavy-duty thread.

11. Refer to **Figure L** as you cut and spread the loops of yarn around the head. Trim the bangs above the eyebrows. Spot glue to keep the hair in place.

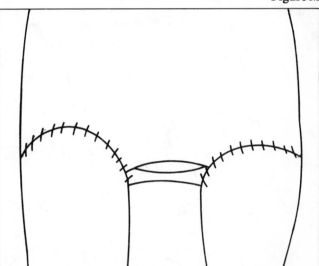

Making the Legs and Shoes

1. Fold one Leg in half lengthwise, placing right sides together. Stitch the seam along the long raw edge, leaving both ends open. Press the seam allowances to the wrong side of the fabric around the open ends. Turn the leg right side out and stuff lightly with fiberfill.

2. Make a second leg in the same manner.

3. To make one shoe, first cut a leg opening in each of two Shoes where indicated on the pattern. These will be the Shoe Tops. Place a Shoe Top and a Shoe Bottom right sides together and stitch the seam all the way around the outer edge. Clip the curves and press the seam allowance to the wrong side of the fabric around the leg opening.

4. Turn the shoe right side out through the opening and stuff lightly with fiberfill.

5. Make a second shoe in the same manner, using the remaining Top and Bottom Shoes.

6. Slip the lower end of a leg into the circular opening on top of one finished shoe. Whipstitch around the edge. Attach the remaining leg and shoe in the same manner.

7. Slip the upper end of one leg into the opening at the lower edge of the body. Whipstitch the leg to the body (**Figure M**). Attach the remaining leg in the same manner, leaving an opening between the legs large enough to stuff the body.

8. Stuff the body with fiberfill. Whipstitch the opening edges together, using heavy-duty thread.

Making the Clown Suit

1. Place one Suit and one Sleeve right sides together and stitch the seam, as shown in **Figure N**. Stitch a second Sleeve to the opposite edge of the same Suit in the same manner. Turn both of the Sleeves outward and press the seam allowances toward the Sleeves.

2. Stitch the remaining two Sleeves to the second Suit in the same manner.

Figure O

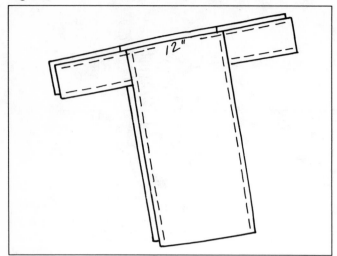

Figure P

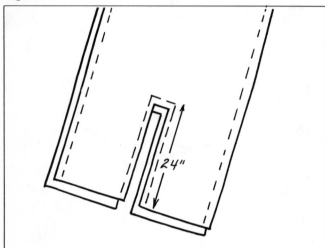

Figure Q

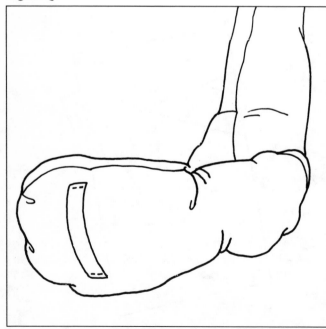

Figure R

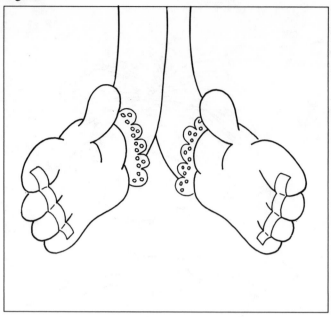

3. Pin the two suit-and-sleeve assemblies right sides together. Stitch the shoulder seams, leaving a 12-inch opening, as shown in **Figure O**. Stitch the underarm and side seam on each side. Press the seam allowances to the wrong side of the fabric along the neck opening. (Do not turn the suit right side out until you've completed step 4.)

4. The suit is divided at the bottom to resemble legs. Measure 24 inches from the lower edge along the vertical center line and mark this point. Run two stitching lines through both layers of the suit from the lower edge to the mark, as shown in **Figure P**. Clip between the two stitching lines. Turn right side out.

5. Hem the raw edges of the sleeves and legs.

6. To make a casing, pin a length of bias tape around each sleeve on the wrong side of the fabric 6 inches from the lower edge. Whipstitch or topstitch both edges of the tape to the sleeve. Overlap the ends of the tape and turn them under.

7. Cut a 5-inch length of elastic and thread it through the casing. Stitch together the ends of the elastic and pull them back inside the casing. Gather the second sleeve and both legs in the same manner.

8. The 7 x 48-inch piece of felt will serve as the ruffle. Stitch the 14-inch piece of elastic lengthwise along the center of the felt, firmly stretching the elastic as you stitch. Be sure to hold both ends of the elastic as you stretch it so you won't break the sewing machine needle. If the elastic won't stretch the full 48 inches, baste lengthwise along the center of the felt and gather to fit the stretched elastic. Stitch the elastic to the felt and remove the basting threads.

9. Place the ruffle around Murphy's neck and tack the ends together at the back.

10. Sew an elastic strip across the bottom of each of Murphy's shoes, attaching only the ends of the elastic (**Figure Q**). To dance with Murphy, just slip your feet under his, using the elastic strips to hold them in place.

11. Glue one layer of the nylon fastener strip to the inside of each of Murphy's hands so he can hug you (**Figure R**).

Spoon Dolls

Turn a pair of wooden kitchen spoons into a delightful doll duo. The spoon dolls are easy to make and the price simply can't be beat. This is a quick and inexpensive project that will please doll collectors from one to ninety-one.

Materials

Two 10-inch wooden kitchen spoons
10 x 21-inch piece of calico fabric
12-inch square of white cotton fabric
6 x 11-inch piece of checked fabric for the knickers
½ yard of unbleached muslin
2½ x 9-inch piece of dark cotton fabric for the suspenders
1 x 2½-inch piece of white felt
6 x 7-inch piece of brown felt
26-inch length of 2½-inch white eyelet trim
29-inch length of ½-inch white lace trim
8-inch length of ⅛-inch white satin ribbon
14-inch length of ⅛-inch satin ribbon to match the calico
8-inch length of ⅜-inch striped trim for the bow tie
Small amounts of yarn in two colors for the hair
Small amount of polyester fiberfill
Non-toxic felt-tip markers in black, blue and red (or acrylic paints and a fine-tipped paint brush)
Hot-melt glue and a glue gun (or white glue)
Flesh-tone thread; white thread; and threads to match the fabrics

Cutting the Pieces

1. Full-size patterns for the Collar, Hat Bill, Arm and Leg are provided in **Figure A**. Trace the patterns onto tracing paper or dressmaker's paper.

2. Scale drawings for the Dress/Shirt, Hat/Bonnet, Apron and Knickers are provided in **Figure B**. Enlarge the drawings to make full-size patterns. (See Tips & Techniques.)

3. Cut the pieces as listed in this step from the various specified fabrics.

Calico:
    Dress – cut two
    Bonnet – cut one

White cotton:
    Apron – cut one
    Shirt – cut two

Brown felt:
    Hat – cut one
    Hat Bill – cut one

White felt:
    Collar – cut one

Checked fabric:
    Knickers – cut two

Unbleached muslin:
    Arm – cut four
    Leg – cut four

Making the Body and Face

Note: The bodies for the boy and girl dolls are identical except for the painted shoes described in step 5. Follow the instructions in this section to make one doll and then repeat to make the second doll. We have allowed a ¼-inch seam allowance on all patterns.

1. Our designs for the facial features are shown in **Figure C**. Use the felt-tip pens or acrylic paints and fine-tipped brush to draw or paint the facial features on the back of the bowl section of each wooden spoon.

2. To make one arm assembly, place two Arms right sides together and stitch the contoured seam, leaving a 2-inch opening for turning and stuffing (**Figure D**). Clip the curves and corners and turn right side out. Press the seam allowances to the inside along the opening. Stuff the arm with fiberfill, using a pencil or similar object to push the stuffing carefully down into the hands. Whipstitch the opening edges together.

3. To soft-sculpt the fingers, use flesh-tone thread and follow

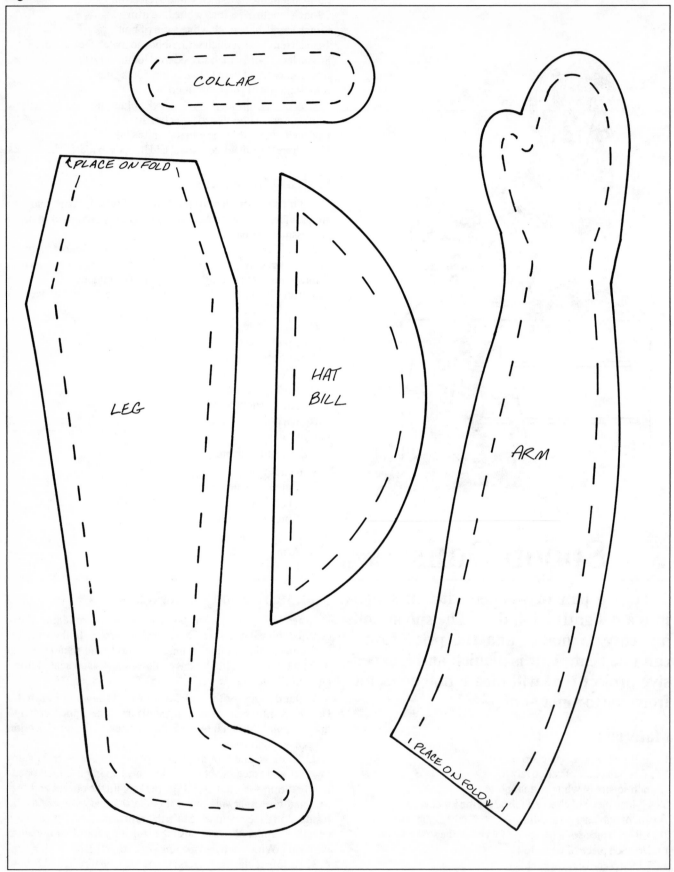

COLLAR

PLACE ON FOLD

LEG

HAT
BILL

ARM

PLACE ON FOLD

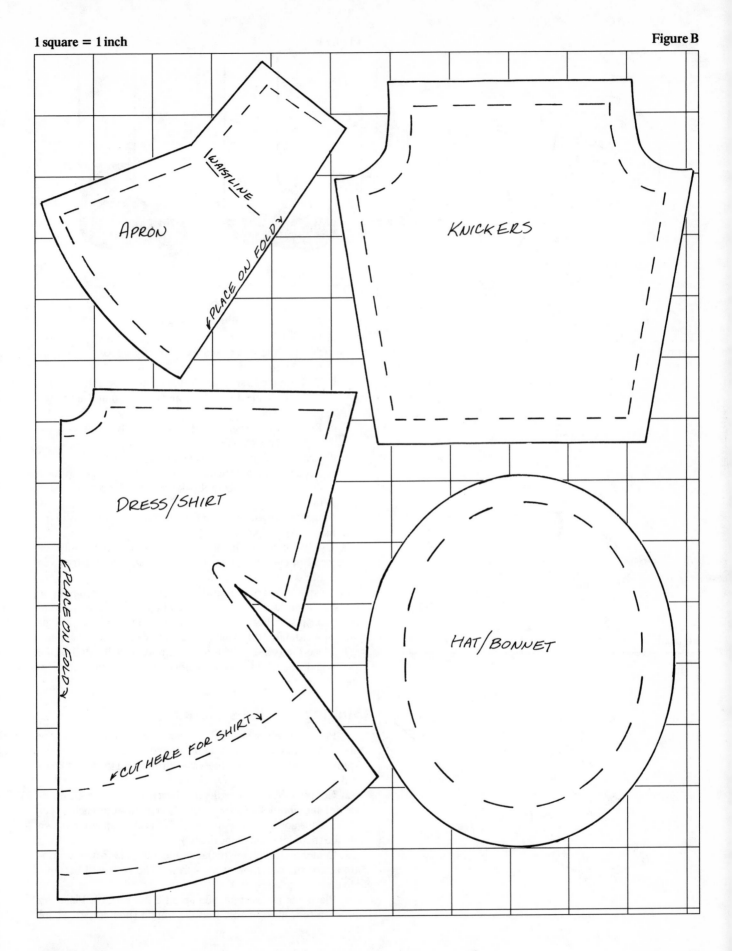

Figure C

Figure D

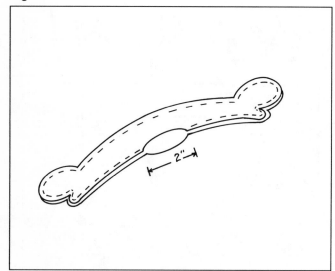

Figure E

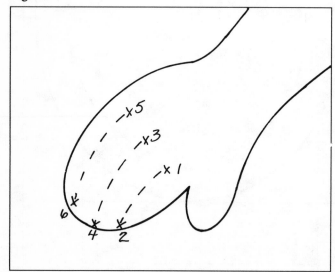

Figure F

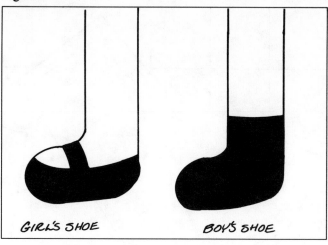

GIRL'S SHOE   BOY'S SHOE

the entry and exit points illustrated in **Figure E**.

   a. Enter at 1 on the palm side of the hand, push the needle through the hand and exit directly opposite 1 on the back of the hand.

   b. To form the first finger, stitch up and down through the hand along the dotted line and exit at point 2 at the end of the finger.

   c. Reenter at 2, push the needle through the hand and exit at point 3 on the palm.

   d. Reenter at 3 on the palm and exit at 3 on the back.

   e. Repeat steps b through d at points 4, 5 and 6, to form the remaining fingers. Lock the stitch at point 6 and cut the thread.

   4. Make the leg assembly in the same manner as you did the arm, using two Leg pieces.

   5. Use black acrylic paint or felt-tip marker to paint a shoe on the end of each leg. The designs we used are illustrated in **Figure F**.

   6. To attach the arms (**Figure G**), place one spoon (bowl side up) on a flat surface. Place the center of the arm assembly across the spoon just below the bowl, making sure that the thumbs point upward. Glue the center of the arm assembly to the spoon.

   7. Place the center of the leg assembly near the end of the spoon and attach it in the same manner as you did the arm (**Figure G**).

Making the Girl's Clothing

   1. Press the Apron seam allowances to the wrong side of the fabric and stitch a narrow hem around the perimeter of the Apron. Stitch a length of white eyelet trim along the lower hemmed edge.

   2. Cut two 1½-inch lengths of ⅛-inch-wide white satin ribbon for the apron shoulder straps. Sew a strap to each upper corner of the apron. (The opposite end of each strap will be sewn into the shoulder seam of the dress.)

   3. Center and stitch the remaining length of narrow satin ribbon across the waistline of the apron. (The ends will be sewn into the dress side seams.)

   4. Place one Dress right side up on a flat surface. Place the apron on top, making sure that the ribbon shoulder straps are

                                                    GREAT FABRIC DOLL BOOK

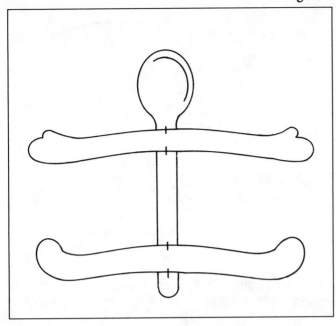

Figure I

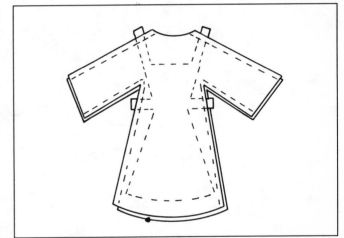

at the shoulder edge and the ribbon waist ties are at the side edges (**Figure H**). Place the second Dress right side down on top of the stack.

5. Stitch the shoulder, underarm and side seams, leaving the neck and lower edges open, as shown in **Figure I**. Clip the corners, press the seam and turn the dress right side out.

6. Stitch lace trim along the end of one sleeve. Gather the sleeve just above the lace, using basting stitches. Repeat for the other sleeve.

7. To put the dress on the girl, you will need to cut a 2-inch slit from the back neck edge down to the center back of the dress. Slip the dress over the girl's head, inserting the arms through the sleeves. Overlap the edges of the slit and glue or whipstitch. Glue lace around the neck for a ruffle.

8. To make the bonnet (**Figure J**), stitch a length of eyelet trim around the edge of the calico Bonnet. Run a line of basting stitches around the edge of the Bonnet, just inside the eyelet. Place a small amount of fiberfill in the center, on the wrong side of the fabric, and pull the basting threads to gather the Bonnet. Tie off the threads and adjust the gathers evenly.

9. The doll's hair consists of braids and bangs. Cut nine 9-inch lengths of yarn. Tie thread tightly around the yarn, close to one end. Braid the strands into one long braid and tie off the other end in the same manner.

10. Tack or glue the center of the braid to the eyelet trim on the bonnet, so each braid points downward (**Figure K**).

11. Cut about thirty 2½-inch lengths of yarn for the bangs. Glue them over the upper edge of the spoon (**Figure L**).

12. Glue the bonnet in place on the back of the spoon. Make a bow, using a strip of calico, and tack or glue it to the lower back edge of the bonnet.

Making the Boy's Clothing

1. Place two Shirts right sides together and stitch the shoulder, underarm and side seams, leaving the sleeve and lower

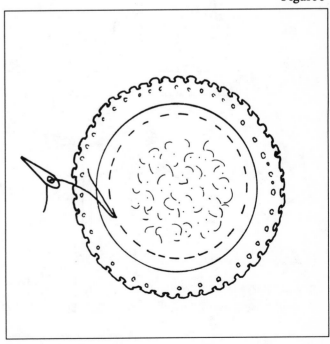

Figure K

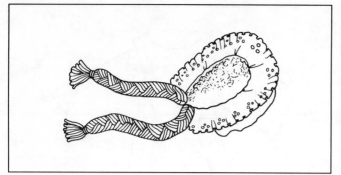

Figure L

Figure M

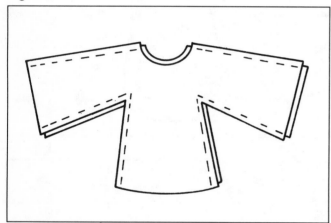

Figure N

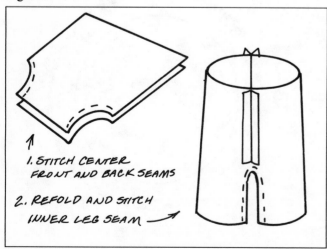

1. STITCH CENTER FRONT AND BACK SEAMS

2. REFOLD AND STITCH INNER LEG SEAM →

Figure O

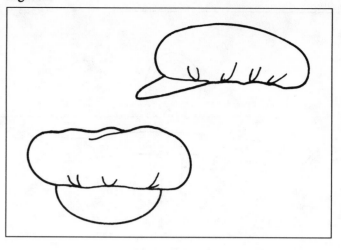

edges open (**Figure M**). Hem the sleeves. Use a contrasting thread to make two straight lines of stitches, approximately ½ inch apart, down the front of the shirt.

2. Place two Knickers right sides together and stitch the curved front and back seams, as shown in **Figure N**. With right sides still together, refold the knickers so that the center front seam matches the center back seam and stitch the inner leg seam. Clip the curves and turn right side out.

3. Sew a narrow hem around the waist and each leg opening. Run a line of basting stitches around the hemmed edge of one leg. Pull the thread to gather the leg slightly and tie off the threads. Gather the other leg in the same manner.

4. Cut a slit from the back neck edge of the shirt, as you did for the dress, and slip the shirt over the doll's head. Turn the raw edges of the slit to the inside. Tack or glue together the top edges of the slit.

5. Cut the 2½ x 9-inch piece of dark cotton fabric in half lengthwise to create two Suspender pieces. Fold one Suspender in half lengthwise, right sides together. Stitch close to the long edge, leaving both ends open. Turn right side out and press. Make another suspender in the same manner.

6. Slip the knickers on the doll and place one suspender over each shoulder. Adjust the length and tack or glue the ends of the suspenders to the inside of the waist.

7. Place the center of the Collar at the center back of the shirt neck edge. Bring the ends of the Collar around to the front and tack or glue in place.

8. Tie the 8-inch length of striped trim into a bow. Glue or tack it to the front of the collar where the edges meet.

9. Cut about twenty 5-inch lengths of yarn for the hair. Glue the yarn across the top edge of the spoon, so that about 2 inches of each strand form the bangs and the remaining 3 inches form the hair.

10. Run a line of basting stitches around the perimeter of the Hat. Place a small amount of fiberfill in the center, on the wrong side of the fabric, and pull the basting thread to gather the Hat slightly. Tie off the threads. Glue or tack the straight edge of the Hat Bill to the gathered edge of the Hat (**Figure O**).

11. Place the hat on the boy's head, with the bill pointing slightly sideways, and glue it in place.

The Old Lady in the Shoe

Here's a favorite nursery rhyme character with an educational purpose. Children will enjoy learning to button, zip and tie with the help of the little old lady, her shoe-shaped house and two of her offspring. The figures range from 5 to 7 inches tall and the shoe towers to a height of 14 inches. When it's naptime, the dolls can be stored inside the shoe.

Materials

1½ yards of calico fabric (We used a yellow print.)
1 yard of quilted gingham fabric that coordinates with the calico (We used green.)
¼ yard of non-quilted gingham fabric that coordinates with the basic color scheme
½ yard of white cotton fabric
¼ yard of muslin or soft flesh-tone fabric
¼ yard of fusible lining fabric
¼ yard of solid-color fabric (We used blue velour.)
1½ yards of 1½-inch-wide satin ribbon (We used red.)
1 yard of 1-inch-wide white eyelet trim
Four white buttons: one ½-inch, one ¾-inch and two ⅜-inch
One package of edge-binding tape (We used green.)
Lengths of assorted ribbon that coordinate with the fabrics
Fabric scraps
Yarn scraps in black, white and orange
7-inch dress zipper
5 x 6-inch piece of 1¼-inch-thick polystyrene foam
Half pound of polyester fiberfill
Half pound of uncooked rice for stuffing the figures

Heavy-duty white thread; regular thread to match the fabrics
Water-soluble fabric marking pen; felt-tip permanent markers for the facial features
Hot-melt glue and a glue gun (or white glue)

Cutting the Pieces

1. Full-size patterns are provided in **Figure A** for the appliques (Shoulder, Body and Hand), and for the Shawl, Boy Foot, Button Tab, Girl/Boy Torso and Arm. Trace the patterns.

2. Scale drawings are provided in **Figure B** for the shoe parts (Toe, Sole, Front Insert, Side, Flap, Heel and Top) and for the Lady Torso. Enlarge the drawings to make full-size paper patterns. (See Tips & Techniques.)

3. Cut the pieces as listed in this step from the specified types and colors of fabric. (**Note:** Use a heated knife to cut the polystyrene heel.)

Calico:
    Shutter – cut four, 3 x 5¼ inches
    Button Tab – cut four
    Door – cut two, 5 x 6½ inches
    Toe – cut two
    Sole – cut two
    Flap – cut four
    Dress – cut one, 5 x 18 inches
    Heel Cover – cut one, 10 x 10 inches

Quilted gingham:
    Shoe Side – cut two

Non-quilted gingham:
    Front Insert – cut one
    Shoe Top – cut one
    Dress – cut one, 4 x 16 inches
    Shawl – cut one

White cotton:
    Window Background – cut one, 5 x 5 inches
    Door – cut one, 5 x 6½ inches
    Cap – cut one, 8-inch-diameter circle

Muslin:
    Head – cut three, 1¾-inch-diameter circle
    Hand – cut one
    Lady Torso – cut two
    Lady Base – cut one, 3½-inch-diameter circle
    Arm – cut six
    Girl Torso – cut two
    Girl Base – cut one, 2¾-inch-diameter circle
    Boy Torso – cut two

Blue velour:
    Shawl – cut one
    Foot – cut four
    Pants – cut two

Fusible lining:
    Window Background – cut one, 4 x 4 inches
    Head – cut three, 1¾-inch-diameter circle
    Shoulder – cut two
    Door – cut one, 5 x 5½ inches
    Hand – cut one
    Body – cut one

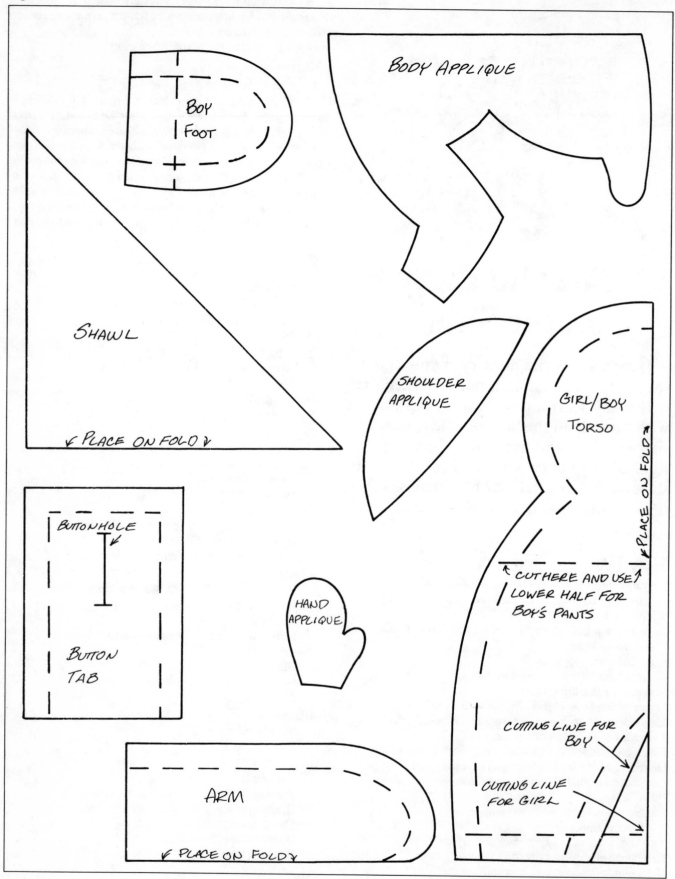

BODY APPLIQUE

BOY
FOOT

SHAWL

← PLACE ON FOLD ↓

SHOULDER
APPLIQUE

GIRL/BOY
TORSO

← PLACE ON FOLD →

BUTTONHOLE

BUTTON
TAB

HAND
APPLIQUE

← CUT HERE AND USE →
LOWER HALF FOR
BOY'S PANTS

CUTTING LINE FOR
BOY

CUTTING LINE
FOR GIRL

ARM

← PLACE ON FOLD ↓

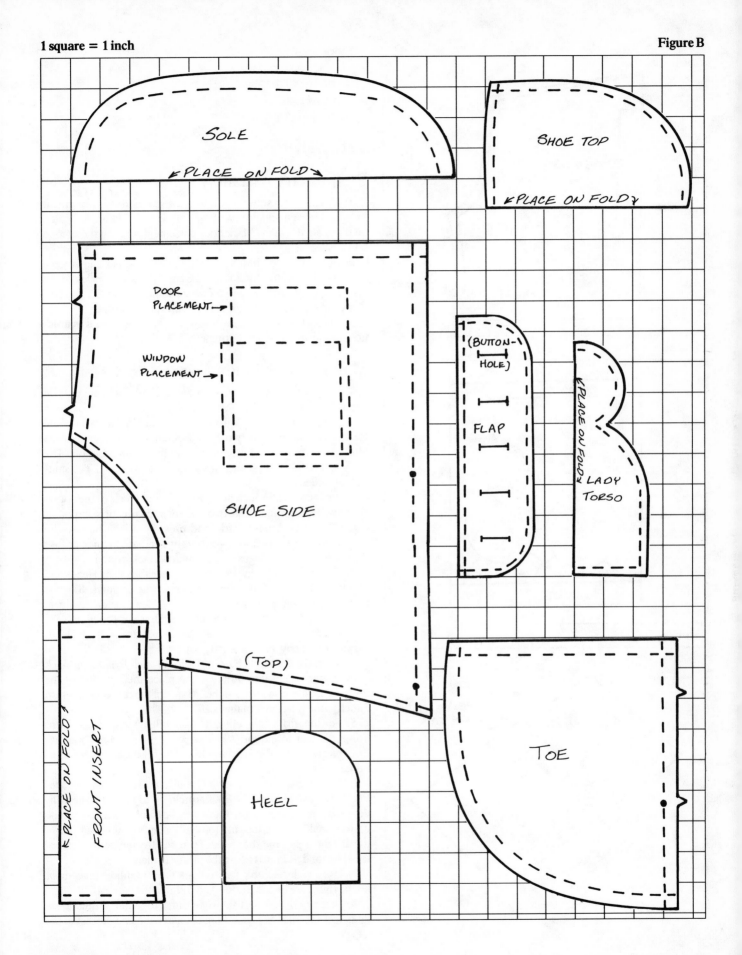

SOLE

←PLACE ON FOLD→

SHOE TOP

←PLACE ON FOLD→

DOOR PLACEMENT →

WINDOW PLACEMENT →

SHOE SIDE

(TOP)

(BUTTON-HOLE)

FLAP

←PLACE ON FOLD→ LADY TORSO

←PLACE ON FOLD→ FRONT INSERT

HEEL

TOE

Figure C

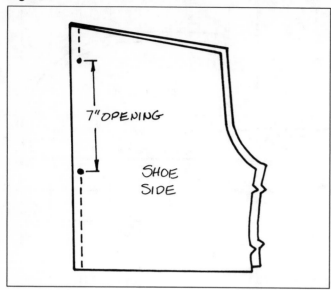

Figure D

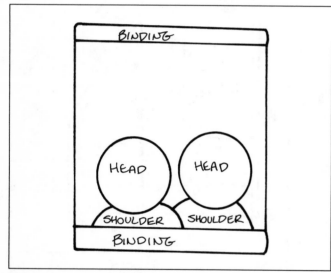

Figure E

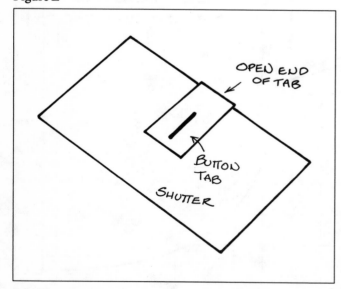

Fabric scraps:
    Shoulder – cut two
    Body – cut one
Polystyrene:
    Heel – cut one

THE SHOE

Preliminary Assembly

1. Use a water-soluble pen to mark the window placement lines on the right side of one fabric Shoe Side, where indicated on the scale drawing. Mark door placement lines on the second fabric Shoe Side.

2. Place the two Shoe Sides right sides together and stitch a ½-inch-wide seam along the back edge (**Figure C**), leaving a 7-inch opening for the zipper where indicated on the pattern. Baste the seam along the zipper opening and press open.

3. Install the zipper according to the manufacturer's instructions. Remove the basting stitches.

Making the Window Scene

We appliqued a window, with two children peeking out, on one side of the shoe. For this section you will need: the cotton and fusible Window Backgrounds, two muslin and two fusible Heads, two fabric and two fusible Shoulders, the four calico Shutters, two calico Button Tabs and the ¾-inch button. The scene is assembled first and then attached to the shoe. The shutters are added last.

1. Press under a ½-inch hem along all four edges of the cotton Window Background. Cut two 4½-inch lengths of seam binding. Open each binding strip and press a ¼-inch hem to the wrong side at each end. Refold the strips and use them to encase the upper and lower edges of the Window Background.

2. To add the children (**Figure D**), place the fabric Heads and Shoulders on top of the fabric Window Background. Slip the matching fusible pieces underneath the Heads and Shoulders and press to fuse, following the manufacturer's instructions.

3. Use felt-tip markers to draw facial features on each Head, making one a boy and one a girl.

4. To make the boy's hair, cut ten 1½-inch lengths of black yarn. Gather them into a bunch and place them on top of the boy's head. Take several stitches to secure the center of the yarn bunch to the top center of the head.

5. For the girl's hair, cut nine 6-inch lengths of black yarn. Stitch the hair to the girl's head at the center and at about ear level on each side. Braid each side and tie off the ends with additional pieces of yarn.

6. Place the shoe-side assembly right side up on a flat surface. Place the fusible Window Background on top, within the window placement markings. Place the assembled window scene on top, making sure that the tops of the appliqued heads point toward the top of the shoe side. Trim any fusible fabric that extends beyond it. Press to fuse the pieces in place.

7. Use a water-soluble pen to mark the buttonhole placement on the right side of one Button Tab (refer to the pattern).

8. Place two Button Tabs right sides together. Stitch a ¼-inch-wide seam along each long edge and the end closest to the

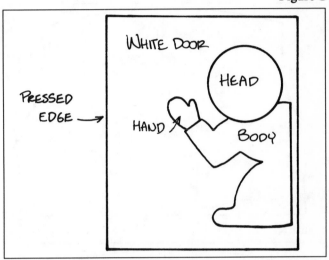

buttonhole marking, leaving the other end open. Clip the corners, turn right side out and press. Work a 1-inch-long buttonhole where indicated.

9. Place one Shutter right side up on a flat surface. Place the assembled button tab on top, as shown in **Figure E**, and pin a second Shutter right side down on top. (The tab will be sandwiched between the two Shutters.) Stitch a ½-inch-wide seam along each edge, leaving an opening large enough for turning. Clip the corners, turn right side out and press. Press the seam allowances to the inside along the opening and topstitch ¼ inch from each edge.

10. Assemble a second shutter in the same manner, omitting the button tab.

11. Pin the shutter with the button tab close to one side of the window, as shown in **Figure F**. Note that the edge including the tab faces center. Blindstitch the shutter to the shoe side along the edge opposite the tab.

12. Stitch the remaining shutter to the opposite side of the window in the same manner. Attach the button to the shutter without the tab, aligning it underneath the buttonhole.

Making the Door Scene

We appliqued to the opposite side of the shoe a door with one child standing and waving. For this section you will need: the white cotton Door, the two calico Doors, the fusible Door, one muslin and one fusible Head, one muslin and one fusible Hand, one fabric and one fusible Body and the ½-inch button.

1. Press under a ½-inch-wide hem along one long edge of the white cotton Door. To add the appliqued child (**Figure G**), match the fusible pieces with the fabric Head, Body and Hand, and place them on the right side of the white Door. The straight edge of the Body should be about ½ inch from the unpressed long edge of the Door. Press to fuse the appliques in place.

2. Use felt-tip markers to draw the facial features, as you did for the window appliques.

3. Cut a 6½-inch length of binding tape and use it to encase the unpressed long edge of the white Door (**Figure H**). Cut two 5-inch lengths of binding tape. Open each one and press a ¼-inch hem to the wrong side at each end. Refold and encase the top and bottom edges of the Door, as shown.

4. To make the boy's hair, cut and attach lengths of black yarn, as you did for the window-applique boy.

5. To make the button tab, follow the same procedures as you did for the first button tab. Work a ¾-inch-long buttonhole where indicated on the pattern.

6. Stitch the button tab to the wrong side of the door at the center of the long encased edge, as shown in **Figure H**.

7. Place the shoe-side assembly right side up on a flat surface. Place the fusible Door on top within the door placement markings. Place the appliqued Door on top, as shown in **Figure I**. Trim the excess fusible fabric and press to fuse.

8. Pin the two calico Doors right sides together. Stitch a ½-inch-wide seam along each edge, leaving an opening large enough for turning. Clip the corners, turn right side out and press. Press the seam allowances to the inside along the opening and topstitch ¼ inch from each edge.

9. Pin the assembled door to the shoe side, close to the unen-

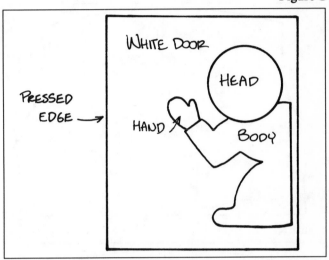

WHITE DOOR

HEAD

PRESSED
EDGE →

HAND

BODY

Figure I

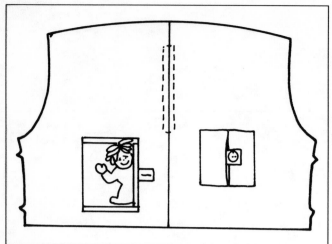

Figure J

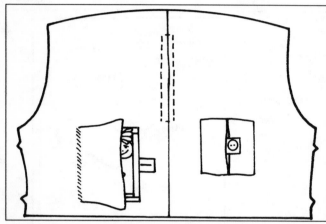

Figure K

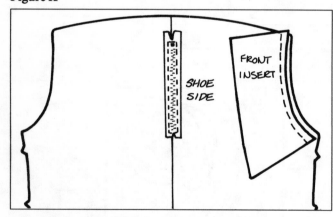

cased edge of the door applique (**Figure J**). Blindstitch the door to the shoe side along that edge only, as shown.

10. Close the door over the appliqued background and fold the button tab over the door. Mark the button placement on the door and stitch the button to the door only.

Finishing the Shoe

To complete this section you will need: the gingham Front

Figure L

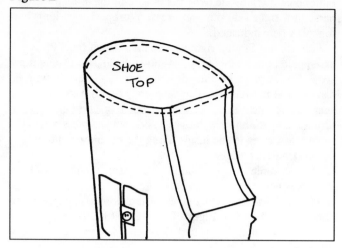

Insert, the gingham Shoe Top, the two calico Soles, the two calico Toes, the four calico Flaps, the polystyrene Heel and the calico Heel Cover. Some of the shoe seams are sewn with the fabrics wrong sides together and the allowances are then encased in binding tape. Pay special attention to the instructions, so you won't have to rip out any seams.

1. Place the shoe-side assembly and the gingham Front Insert *wrong* sides together (**Figure K**), aligning one long edge of the Insert with the curved front edge of one shoe side. Ease the Insert to fit and stitch a ¼-inch-wide seam. Stitch the opposite long edge of the Insert to the curved front edge of the other shoe side in the same manner. Encase the seam allowances.

2. Pin the Shoe Top to the upper edge of the shoe assembly, placing *wrong* sides together (**Figure L**). Stitch a ¼-inch-wide seam and encase the seam allowances.

3. Place the two Shoe Toes right sides together, matching notches. Stitch a ½-inch-wide seam along the long curved edge only. Clip the curve and press the seam open. Open the two sections and run a line of basting stitches between the two dots (**Figure M**). Pull the thread to gather the edge.

4. The assembled toe is now attached to the shoe, but this step is a bit tricky. At the toe end of the shoe Front Insert, fold the bound edges toward each other forming a pleat on each side, so that the bound edges are about 1 inch apart. Pin together the front notched edge of the shoe assembly and the gathered edge of the toe, with right sides together and notches matching, as shown in **Figure N**. Ease the gathers to fit, placing the toe seam at the center of the Front Insert. Stitch a ½-inch-wide toe-to-shoe seam, clip the curves and press.

5. Pin the two Soles *wrong* sides together. Stitch a ½-inch-wide seam all the way around, leaving an opening large enough for stuffing. Stuff the sole lightly and stitch the opening. Encase the seam allowances.

6. Baste around the lower edge of the shoe. Gather the edge so that is it slightly smaller than the sole. Pin the sole to the bottom of the shoe, tucking the gathered raw edge of the shoe to the inside. Blindstitch the shoe to the sole.

7. Use the water-soluble pen to mark the placement of five buttonholes on the right side of two Flaps, where indicated on the pattern. To assemble one flap, place a marked and an unmarked Flap right sides together. Stitch a ¼-inch-wide seam

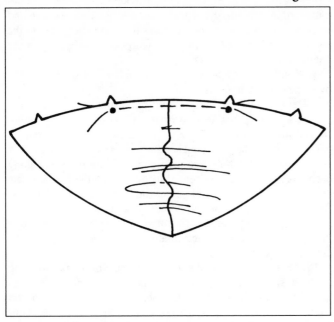

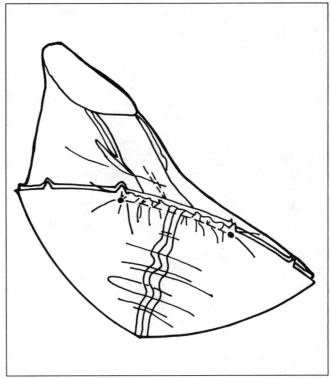

along each edge, leaving an opening for turning. Clip the curves and corners, turn right side out and press. Press the seam allowances to the inside along the opening and stitch closed.

8. Work the buttonholes where indicated.

9. Pin the straight edge of the flap to the assembled shoe about ¼ inch behind one bound edge of the front insert, as shown in **Figure O**. Blindstitch in place along the straight edge.

10. Repeat steps 7 and 8 to assemble a second flap. Attach it to the opposite side of the shoe in the same manner.

11. Place the calico Heel Cover wrong side up on a flat surface and center the polystyrene Heel on top. Wrap the fabric up over the edges of the Heel to the top, smoothing out the wrinkles as you go. Glue the fabric edges to the top of the Heel.

12. The heel is attached to the shoe, as shown in **Figure P**. Place the top of the heel against the shoe sole where indicated and glue in place.

13. To make a shoestring, fold the 1½-inch-wide satin ribbon in half lengthwise, placing right sides together. Stitch a ¼-inch-wide seam along the entire length, leaving both ends open. Turn right side out. Press the raw edges to the inside at each end and blindstitch the ends closed.

14. Lace the shoestring through the buttonholes in the shoe flaps. Tie the ends in a big bow.

THE DOLLS

The Old Lady

To complete this section you will need: the two muslin Lady Torsos, two muslin Arms, the muslin Lady Base, the calico Dress, the blue velour Shawl and the white cotton Cap.

1. Place the two Lady Torsos right sides together and stitch a continuous ¼-inch-wide seam along the contoured edge (**Figure Q**). Leave the lower edge open, as shown. Clip the curves and corners and turn right side out.

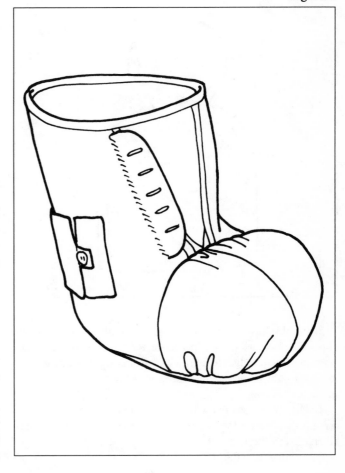

Figure P

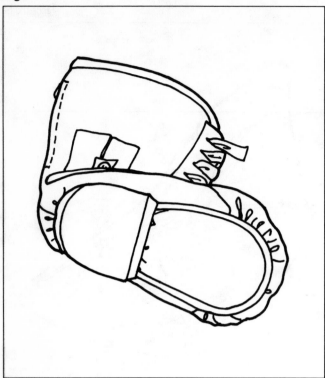

Figure Q

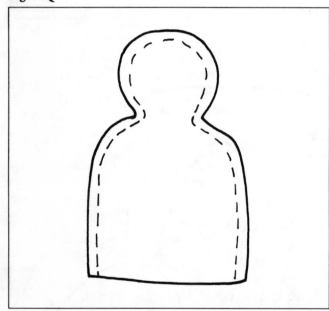

2. Pin the Base to the lower edge of the torso, placing right sides together, as shown in **Figure R**. Stitch a ¼-inch-wide seam around the edge, leaving a 3-inch opening. Clip the curves and turn right side out. Press the seam allowances to the inside along the opening.

3. The torso is stuffed with fiberfill and uncooked rice to add weight. Stuff the head and the upper portion of the torso with fiberfill. Fill the rest of the torso with rice and blindstitch the opening edges together.

4. Fold one Arm in half along the "place on fold" line with right sides together. Stitch a ¼-inch-wide seam along the contoured edge, leaving the straight end open. Clip the curve and corners, turn right side out and press the seam allowance to the inside around the open end. Stuff with fiberfill right up to the open end.

5. Blindstitch the arm to the assembled torso, centering it over one of the side seams.

6. Repeat steps 4 and 5 to assemble and attach a second arm.

7. Use felt-tip markers to draw the facial features. Stitch twelve short strands of white yarn to the front of the forehead to form bangs. The rest of the head will be covered by a cap.

8. Press a ¼-inch hem to the wrong side of the fabric along each edge of the calico Dress. Machine stitch the hems. Baste close to one long edge and gather the fabric so that it will just fit around the stuffed torso underneath the arms.

9. Wrap the dress around the torso, placing the gathered edge just beneath the arms. Tack together the upper corners of the dress at the back.

10. Press a ¼-inch hem to the wrong side of the fabric along the longest edge of the velour Shawl and stitch in place. Pin eyelet trim to the right side of the Shawl along the two shorter edges, as shown in **Figure S**. For a decorative touch, use contrasting thread to stitch the eyelet in place. Turn under the raw ends of the eyelet.

11. Overlap the front corners of the shawl and tack them together. Cut a 6-inch length of ribbon and tie it into a small bow. Tack the bow to the right side of the shawl, over the lapped ends. (This will be the front of the shawl.) Slip the completed shawl over the old lady's head.

12. Turn and press a ¼-inch hem to the wrong side of the fabric all the way around the Cap. Pin eyelet trim around the edge, as shown in **Figure T**. Use contrasting thread to stitch the eyelet in place, as you did for the shawl.

13. Baste around the cap about 1 inch from the hemmed edge of the fabric. Place a small ball of fiberfill in the center of the cap on the wrong side and gather the cap around the fiberfill. Adjust the gathers to fit the old lady's head and whipstitch the cap in place along the gathering line.

The Girl

To complete this section you will need: the two muslin Girl Torsos, two muslin Arms, the muslin Girl Base, the gingham Dress and the gingham Shawl.

1. Assemble the girl's body in the same manner as you did the old lady's except for the hair. Use felt-tip markers to draw the facial features.

2. To make the hair, cut twelve 8-inch lengths of orange yarn. Gather the strands into a bunch. Stitch the center of the bunch to the top of the girl's head and stitch the yarn to the head at about ear level on each side. Braid the yarn on each side and tie off the ends of the braids with pieces of the same color yarn. If you wish, you can glue or stitch small scraps of yarn to the forehead to form bangs. Tie a small ribbon bow around each braid over the yarn tie.

3. Make and attach the girl's gingham dress in the same manner as you did the old lady's.

4. The girl's shawl is made in the same manner, omitting the eyelet trim. Press a ¼-inch hem to the wrong side of the fabric

Romeo Scarecrow
page 82

Callie & Caleb
page 90

Caleb
page 90

Callie
page 90

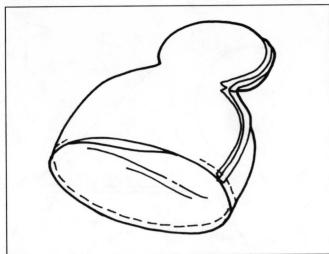

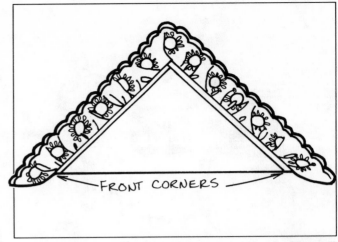

FRONT CORNERS

along each edge of the Shawl and stitch. Drape the shawl around the girl's shoulders, overlapping the front corners. Tack together the front corners and tack them to the front of the dress. Stitch or glue a small ribbon bow over the stitches.

The Boy

To complete this section you will need: the two muslin Boy Torsos, the two remaining muslin Arms, the four blue velour Feet, the two blue velour Pants and the two ⅜-inch buttons.

1. Assemble the two arms in the same manner as you did for the old lady's.

2. Pin two Foot pieces right sides together. Stitch a ¼-inch-wide seam along the curved edge, leaving the straight end open. Clip the curves and turn right side out. Make a second foot in the same manner.

3. Baste both feet to the right side of one Boy Torso (**Figure U**). Pin the second Torso right side down on top (the feet will be sandwiched between). Stitch a ¼-inch-wide seam all the way around, leaving an opening large enough for turning. Clip the curves and corners, turn right side out and press the seam allowances to the inside along the opening. Stuff the top of the torso with fiberfill and the lower portion with rice. Blindstitch the opening edges together.

4. Blindstitch the two arms to the torso.

5. Use felt-tip markers to draw facial features. Glue scraps of black yarn to the head for hair.

6. Place the two Pants right sides together and stitch the seams, leaving the waist edge and the leg ends unstitched. Clip the inseam and turn right side out. Stitch a narrow hem around the waist and leg edges. Glue or stitch the two ⅜-inch buttons to the front waist edge, centering the buttons directly above the two pant legs.

7. Slip the pants onto the body. Cut two 4-inch lengths of co-ordinating ribbon for the suspenders. To make one suspender, glue one end of the ribbon to the inside of the pants at the back waist edge directly above one leg. Drape the ribbon over the shoulder opposite the leg and glue the front end to the front waist edge behind the button. Attach the second ribbon suspender in the same manner.

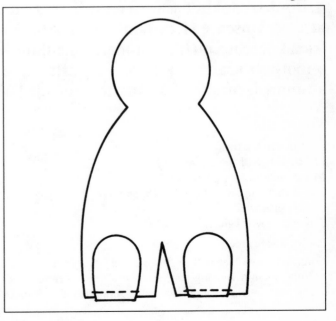

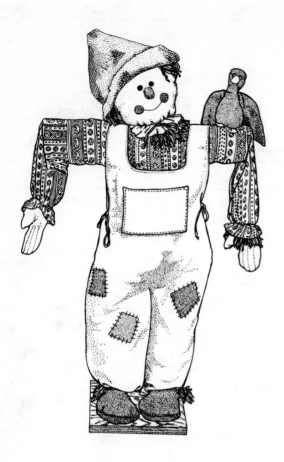

Romeo Scarecrow

Romeo couldn't scare a crow if he tried, just ask Unscared Crow, his little feathered friend perched on his shoulder. This almost 4-foot-tall scarecrow makes an attractive autumn decoration for your home or yard.

Materials

For the wooden frame:

12-inch length of 1 x 12 pine

24-inch length of 1 x 2 pine

Two 3-foot lengths and one 7-inch length of ⅝-inch-diameter wooden dowel rod

Carpenter's wood glue

For Romeo Scarecrow:

Note: We have included in this list the fabrics required for Romeo's shirt, overalls and hat. As you'll see when you read the instructions, we have greatly simplified the designs

of these items, so they are far easier to assemble than normal wearable versions would be. If you prefer, you can scrounge the clothing from your "giveaway" pile or purchase it at a garage sale or thrift shop.

1 yard of 36-inch cotton print fabric for the shirt

1¼ yards of 36-inch denim fabric (or 1 yard of 44-inch fabric) for the overalls

Scraps of felt or other fabric for the patches on the overalls (We used 3½-inch-square pieces in red, yellow and gold.)

¾ yard of 36-inch lightweight white or flesh-tone cotton fabric for the head and hands

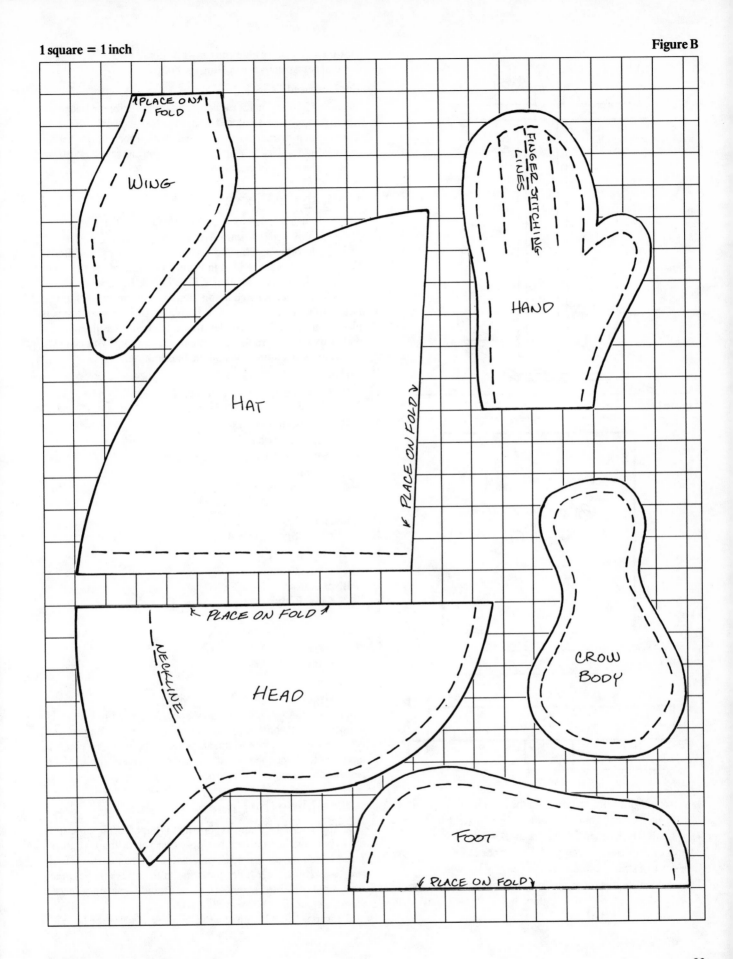

PLACE ON FOLD

WING

FINGER STITCHING LINES

HAND

HAT

PLACE ON FOLD

CROW BODY

PLACE ON FOLD

NECKLINE

HEAD

FOOT

PLACE ON FOLD

Figure C

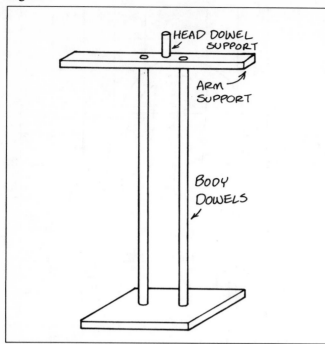

Figure D

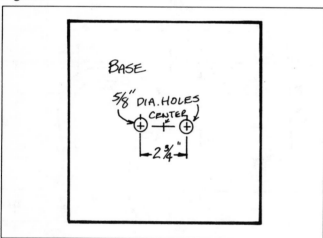

Figure E

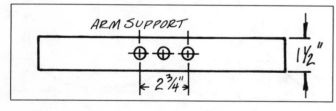

⅜ yard of 36-inch brown fabric for the feet and nose
14 x 28-inch piece of burlap or other fabric for the hat
Two small scraps of red felt for the cheek spots
2 yards of ⅛-inch-diameter white cotton cord
One skein of straw-colored rug yarn (or real straw)
Two ⅝-inch-diameter fabric-covered dome buttons for the eyes
A long sharp needle; heavy-duty black thread; and regular thread to match the fabrics

Hot-melt glue and a glue gun (or white glue)
Several newspapers for stuffing the body

For Unscared Crow:
⅜ yard of 36-inch medium-weight black fabric for the body
Small scraps of gold-colored felt for the feet and beak
Two ⅜-inch-diameter white domed shank-type buttons for the eyes; and a black felt-tip marker (Or you can purchase plastic eyes at a hobby or craft shop.)

Cutting the Pieces

1. Full-size patterns for the Beak, Crow Feet, Cheek Spot and Nose are provided in **Figure A**. Trace the patterns.
2. Scale drawings for the Hand, Foot, Head, Crow Body, Wing and Hat are provided in **Figure B**. Enlarge the drawings to make full-size paper patterns. (See Tips & Techniques.)
3. Cut the pieces listed in this step from the specified fabrics. **Note:** Romeo doesn't have a body, as such; his clothing is placed on the padded wooden frame to create the illusion of a real body. If you are using ready-made clothing, you can skip the sections on cutting and making the clothing.

Cotton print:
  Shirt – cut two, 11 x 16 inches
  Sleeve – cut two, 14 x 21 inches
White or flesh-tone cotton:
  Head – cut two
  Hand – cut four
Brown fabric:
  Foot – cut four
  Nose – cut one
Red felt:
  Cheek Spot – cut two
Burlap:
  Hat – cut one
Black cotton:
  Crow Body – cut two
  Wing – cut two
Gold felt:
  Beak – cut one
  Crow Feet – cut one
Denim:
  Overalls – cut two, 22 x 36 inches

4. The two Overalls must be shaped, as shown in **Figure F**. Trim one, but don't worry about being exact as long as you come reasonably close to the shape. Use the trimmed piece as a pattern to shape the second. Save the 5½ x 6-inch bib cutout from one and label it as the Pocket.

Assembling the Frame

1. The assembled frame is shown in **Figure C**. It is quite simple to put together and requires only that you drill a few holes. The 12-inch length of 1 x 12 pine will serve as the Base. Drill two ⅝-inch-diameter holes through the Base, 2¾ inches apart (measured center to center). The holes should be evenly spaced from the center, as shown in **Figure D**.
2. Insert a 3-foot length of dowel into each hole in the Base.

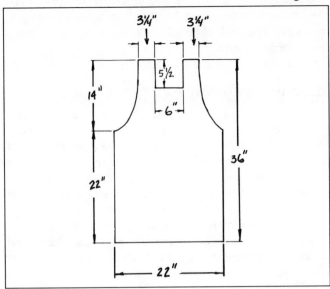

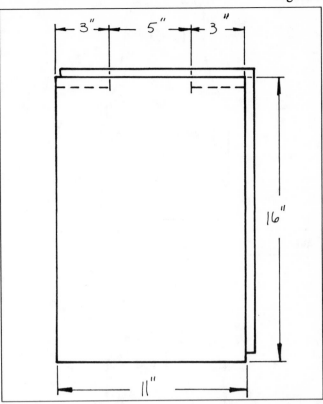

The lower end of each dowel should be flush with the underside of the Base. Leave the dowels unglued.

3. The 24-inch length of 1 x 2 pine will serve as the Arm Support. It must be drilled (**Figure E**) to accommodate the long body dowels and the short head-support dowel. Drill a ⅝-inch-diameter hole at the center point. Drill two additional ⅝-inch holes, each 1⅜ inches from the center, one on either side.

4. To install the Arm Support on the frame, insert the upper ends of the 3-foot-long dowels into the outer holes in the Arm Support. The upper ends of these dowels should be flush with the upper surface of the Arm Support and they should be left unglued for the time being. Insert and glue the 7-inch length of dowel down into the center hole of the Arm Support. The lower end of the head-support dowel should be flush with the underside of the Arm Support. Your assembled frame should now look like the diagram in **Figure C**.

Making the Shirt

Note: All seam allowances are ½ inch wide unless otherwise specified in the instructions.

1. Place the two Shirts right sides together and stitch the shoulder seams, as shown in **Figure G**. Be sure to leave a 5-inch neck opening at the center, as shown. Press the seams open and press the seam allowances to the wrong side of the fabric along the neck opening.

2. Open out the shirt front and back and place the assembly right side up on a flat surface. Place one of the Sleeves right side down on top, as shown in **Figure H**, aligning one end of the Sleeve with one side edge of the shirt assembly. The lengthwise center line of the Sleeve should be aligned over the shoulder seam of the shirt. Stitch together the Sleeve and shirt, as shown. Press the seam open and turn the sleeve outward.

3. Stitch the remaining Sleeve to the opposite side edge of the shirt in the same manner.

4. Fold the shirt right sides together and stitch the underarm and side seam on each side, as shown in **Figure I**. Press the seams open.

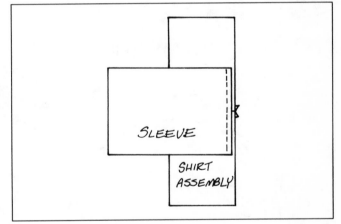

Figure I

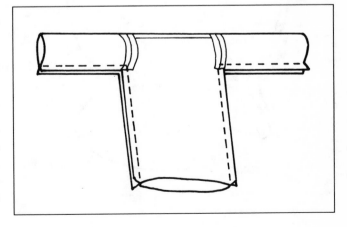

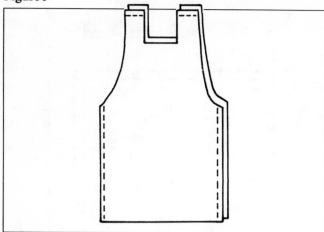

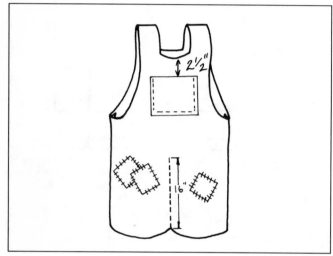

Figure L

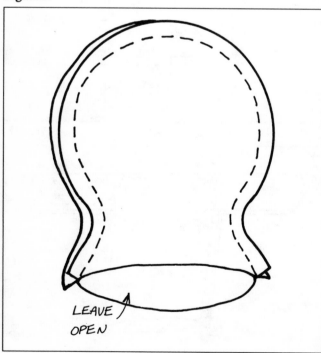

LEAVE OPEN

5. Press and stitch a narrow hem around the open lower end of each sleeve. Baste about 2 inches from the hemmed edge. Do not cut off the tails of thread, as the sleeves will be gathered around the hands later.

6. Hem the lower edge of the shirt.

Making the Overalls

1. Turn and press a ½-inch hem to the wrong side of the fabric along all four edges of the Pocket. Machine stitch the hem along one long edge only. Pin the pocket, right side up, to the right side of one Overalls piece. The stitched long edge of the pocket should be centered about 2½ inches below the lower edge of the bib cutout. Topstitch the pocket in place close to each side edge and the lower edge, leaving the upper edge open.

2. Arrange several patches on the right side of one or both Overalls. We glued the patches in place and then drew "stitches" along the edges, using a black marker; you may prefer to stitch them in place by hand or machine.

3. Place the two Overalls right sides together and stitch the shoulder and side seams, as shown in **Figure J**. Press open.

4. Turn and press a ½-inch hem to the wrong side of the fabric along all open raw edges of the overalls (the bib, armhole and lower edges); you'll have to clip the hem allowances at the corners and curves to make the hems lie flat. Machine stitch the hems and turn the overalls right side out.

5. To divide the lower portion of the overalls and create the illusion of two legs, topstitch through the front and back layers from the center of the lower edge upward, as shown in **Figure K**. The stitching line should be about 16 inches long.

6. Baste around the open lower end of each leg section about 1 inch from the hemmed edge. Do not cut off the tails of thread.

Making the Head

1. Place the two Heads right sides together and stitch the seam along the long contoured edge, leaving the lower edge open (**Figure L**). Clip the curves and turn right side out.

2. Hem the open lower edge of the head. Baste around the neckline where indicated on the pattern. Do not cut off the tails of thread.

3. Stuff the head firmly with fiberfill. Do not stuff below the neckline. Pull the neckline basting threads to gather the fabric slightly and hold the stuffing in place; do not pull tightly, but rather just enough to keep the stuffing from falling out and to create a neck indentation. Tie off the gathering threads and adjust the gathers evenly.

4. Baste around the Nose about ¼ inch from the edge. Place a small wad of fiberfill in the center of the Nose, on the wrong side of the fabric, and pull up the basting threads to gather the fabric around the stuffing. Tie off the threads securely.

5. Romeo's head, with facial features in place, is shown in **Figure M**. Glue or whipstitch the nose to one side of Romeo's head at the approximate center. Be sure that the gathered side of the nose is placed against the face. Glue or stitch the two button eyes in place, as shown.

6. To create Romeo's winning smile, thread a long needle

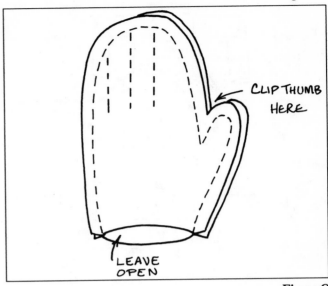

with heavy-duty black thread and follow the entry and exit points illustrated in **Figure M**.

    a. Enter at point 1 (about ¾ inch below the nose and 1 inch to the right).

    b. Push the needle through the stuffing inside the head and exit at 2 (about 1¼ inches below the center of the nose).

    c. Pull the thread across the surface, enter at 3 and exit at point 2.

    d. Pull the thread across the surface and enter at 1.

    e. Repeat all of the procedures in steps b, c and d two more times, pulling gently to indent the mouth lines. Lock the final stitch at point 1 and cut the thread.

  7. Glue or whipstitch the two Cheek Spots to Romeo's face over the corners of the mouth, as shown.

Making the Hands, Feet and Hat

  1. Place two Hands right sides together and stitch the seam along the long contoured edge, leaving the straight wrist end open (**Figure N**). Clip the curves and the inside corner at the base of the thumb. Turn right side out.

  2. Stuff lightly with fiberfill. To sculpt the fingers, topstitch through the hand along each dotted finger line, as shown in **Figure N** and on the pattern.

  3. Repeat steps 1 and 2 to create a second hand.

  4. Place two Foot pieces right sides together and stitch the seam all the way around the edge, leaving the heel end open, as shown in **Figure O**. Clip the curves and turn right side out. Press the seam allowances to the inside along the opening.

  5. Stuff the foot firmly with fiberfill and whipstitch the opening edges together.

  6. Repeat steps 4 and 5 to create a second foot.

  7. Fold the Hat right sides together along the "place on fold" line indicated on the pattern. Stitch the seam along the aligned straight edges, leaving the curved lower edge open (**Figure P**). Press the seam open and turn right side out. Baste about 2½ inches from the raw lower edge. Do not cut off the tails of thread. Hem the lower edge of the hat.

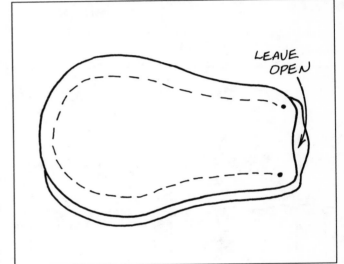

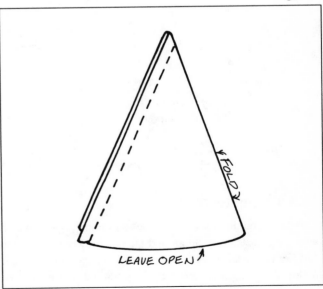

ROMEO SCARECROW

Figure Q

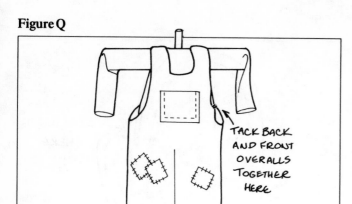

TACK BACK AND FRONT OVERALLS TOGETHER HERE

Figure R

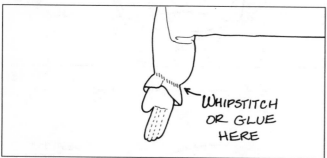

WHIPSTITCH OR GLUE HERE

Figure S

Figure T

Figure U

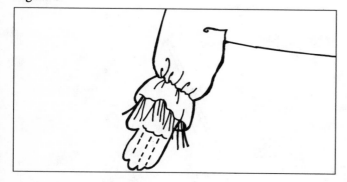

Assembling Romeo

Note: If you did not make Romeo's clothing, but are using old clothes instead, baste around the open lower end of each shirt sleeve about 2 inches from the edge. Do not cut off the tails of thread. In the same manner, baste around the lower end of each pants leg about 1 inch from the edge; and baste around the hat about 2½ inches from the edge of the brim.

1. Glue wadded newspaper to the wooden frame, leaving uncovered the head-support dowel and about 2 inches at the lower end of each body dowel. Keep in mind that the body dowels must be removed to dress the form so separate the stuffing between the frame members.

2. Temporarily remove the body dowels from the base and arm support. Slip the arm support inside the shirt so that the head-support dowel extends up through the neck opening and one sleeve hangs over each end. Insert a body dowel into each overalls leg. Spread wood glue around the lower end of each body dowel and reinsert the dowels into the base. Place the shirted arm support above the body dowels and insert one end of the arm support through each overall strap. Pull up the bottom of the shirt, spread glue around the upper end of each body dowel and insert the dowels up into the holes in the arm support. Tuck the shirt down into the overalls.

3. If you wish, you can add more stuffing inside the body, the legs and the upper portions of the sleeves.

4. On one side of the overalls, tack together the front and back layers close to the stuffed shirt at about waist level, as shown in **Figure Q**. Cut an 18-inch length of cotton cord, tie a large bow at the center and stitch the bow to the overalls over the tacking stitches. The corner of the overalls that extends out beyond the tacking stitches can be tucked inside to create a side pocket. Repeat these procedures to close the overalls waist on the opposite side.

5. Pull up the basting threads to gather the lower end of one leg, leaving an opening about 2 inches in diameter. Tie off the threads and adjust the gathers evenly. Lift the lower end of one leg and insert the heel end of a foot underneath it. The back of the foot should rest against the body dowel and the toe end should extend out over the base, facing the same direction as the front of the overalls. Glue the foot to the base. Lower the leg so that it rests on top of the foot and glue or whipstitch the leg to the foot along the gathering threads. Repeat these procedures to attach the second foot to the other leg.

6. The hands are attached next. We left unstuffed the portion of each sleeve that extends beyond the arm support. Insert the open wrist end of a hand into the open lower end of one sleeve; make sure that the thumb faces the same direction as the front of the overalls when the arm is allowed to hang downward naturally. Pull up the basting threads to gather the sleeve around the wrist and tie off the threads. Adjust the gathers evenly. Glue or whipstitch the hand to the sleeve along the gathering threads (**Figure R**). Attach the remaining hand to the other sleeve in the same manner, turning it so the thumb faces front.

7. To attach Romeo's head, place it above the head-support dowel, making sure that the face points in the same direction as the front of the overalls. Make a narrow cavity in the head stuffing and lower the head down over the dowel. Manipulate the head so that the gathered neckline rests on the shirt (**Figure S**). Pull up the neckline gathering threads, if necessary, to create a more defined neck. Glue or whipstitch the head to the shirt around the neckline. Wrap the remaining cotton cord around the neckline and tie it in a bow at the front.

8. You may wish to stuff the hat lightly or leave it unstuffed. To attach the hat, pull up the basting threads and adjust the gathers evenly so that it fits Romeo's head, as shown in **Figure T**. The hat should be turned with the seam at the back. Tie off the gathering threads and glue or whipstitch the hat to Romeo's head along the gathering threads.

9. We used straw-colored yarn to create the illusion of straw, but you may have opted to use real straw. If you are using real straw, gather up small bunches and glue them around each hand underneath the ends of the sleeves so that the straw extends outward (**Figure U**). Follow the same procedures to glue bunches of straw around the top of each shoe underneath the ends of the legs, around the neck underneath the edge of the head fabric and around the upper portion of the head underneath the hat brim. If you are using yarn, you'll have to cut it into shorter lengths. Gather several lengths together to create small bunches, tie each bunch together at the center and then glue or whipstitch them to the body, as described for the straw.

Making Unscared Crow

1. Place the two Crow Bodies right sides together and stitch the seam all the way around the edge, leaving an opening at the lower end, as shown in **Figure V**. Clip the curves and turn right side out. Press the seam allowances to the inside along the opening edges.

2. Stuff the body very firmly with fiberfill and whipstitch the opening edges together.

3. Place the two Wings right sides together and stitch the seam all the way around the edge, leaving a short opening (**Figure W**). Clip the curves and corners and turn right side out. Press the seam allowances to the inside along the opening edges. We did not stuff the wings, but you may stuff them lightly with fiberfill, if you prefer. Whipstitch the opening edges together.

4. Place the wings across the stuffed crow body, as shown in **Figure X**, and glue or whipstitch them in place.

5. Fold the Beak in half and stitch a very narrow seam along the longer straight edge, leaving the shorter edge open (**Figure Y**). Clip the corner and turn right side out. Stuff.

6. Figure Z shows the facial features attached. Place the beak against the head, on the side of the body opposite the wings, and glue or whipstitch it in place. To create indentations for the eyes, pinch up a narrow vertical ridge just above the beak and take a few hand stitches back and forth underneath the ridge, pulling the thread gently. Continue working with the same thread to stitch an eye button over each indentation. If you are using plastic eyes, glue one into each indentation. If you used buttons, draw an upper eyelid and pupil on each button, using the black felt-tip marker (**Figure AA**).

7. To divide the toes on each foot portion of the Crow Feet, make a straight cut from the toe end in toward the center along each clip line indicated on the pattern (**Figure BB**). Place the assembled body on top of the clipped feet, making sure that the toes extend outward from the front of the body. Glue or whipstitch the center of the feet to the bottom of the body.

8. Place Unscared Crow on one of Romeo's shoulders and glue or whipstitch him in place.

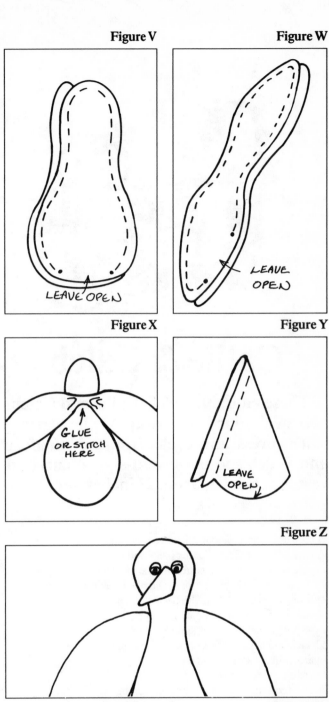

Figure V   Figure W

LEAVE OPEN

LEAVE OPEN

Figure X   Figure Y

GLUE OR STITCH HERE

LEAVE OPEN

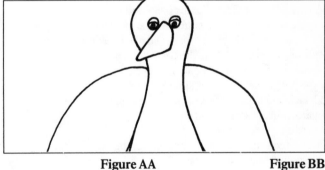

Figure Z

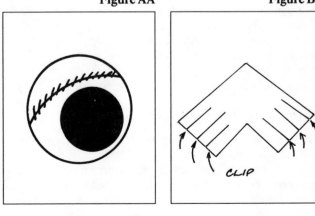

Figure AA   Figure BB

CLIP

Callie & Caleb

These adorable twins, Callie and Caleb, will steal your heart away. Callie wears a calico dress and eyelet-trimmed pinafore and Caleb sports western-style chaps and vest. Each doll is about 21 inches tall.

Materials

¾ yard of brown calico for the dress and shirt
½ yard of brown fleece for the pants and vest
½ yard of ivory-colored cotton for the pinafore and bloomers
9 x 12-inch piece each of brown and black felt for the shoes
2 yards of unbleached muslin for the doll bodies
1¾ yards of 1-inch ivory gathered eyelet trim
2 yards of 1-inch ivory grosgrain ribbon
20-inch length of ½-inch brown grosgrain ribbon
1 yard of beige single-fold tape
1 yard of ¼-inch elastic
Four 1-inch-diameter black buttons for the eyes
One pound of polyester fiberfill
Long sharp needle; heavy-duty thread in flesh-tone and black; and regular thread to match the fabrics
One skein of red rug yarn for the hair
Red embroidery floss
Cosmetic cheek blusher
A black fine-point felt-tip marker

Cutting the Pieces

1. Full-size patterns are provided in **Figure A** for the Nose and Shoe. Trace the patterns.

2. Scale drawings are provided in **Figures B** and **C** for the Leg, Arm, Torso Bottom, Boot, Vest, Shirt Sleeve, Dress Sleeve, Bodice, Head, Torso, Pants, Shirt Back, Shirt Front,

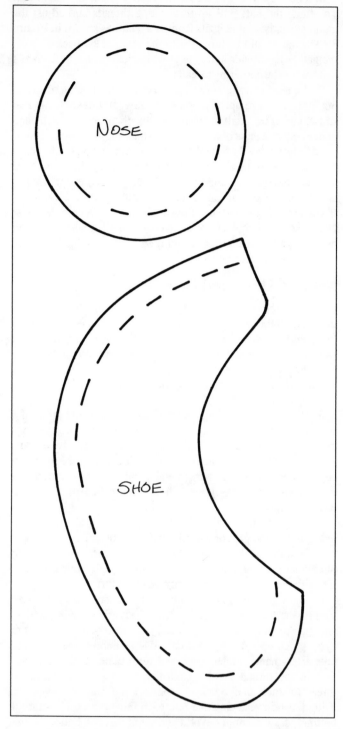

Bloomers and Pinafore. Enlarge the drawings to make full-size paper patterns. (Refer to Tips & Techniques.)

3. Cut the pieces as listed in this step from the specified fabrics. **Note:** The cutting instructions for the muslin body pieces are for *one* doll. Repeat the instructions for the second doll.

Muslin:
    Torso – cut two
    Torso Bottom – cut one

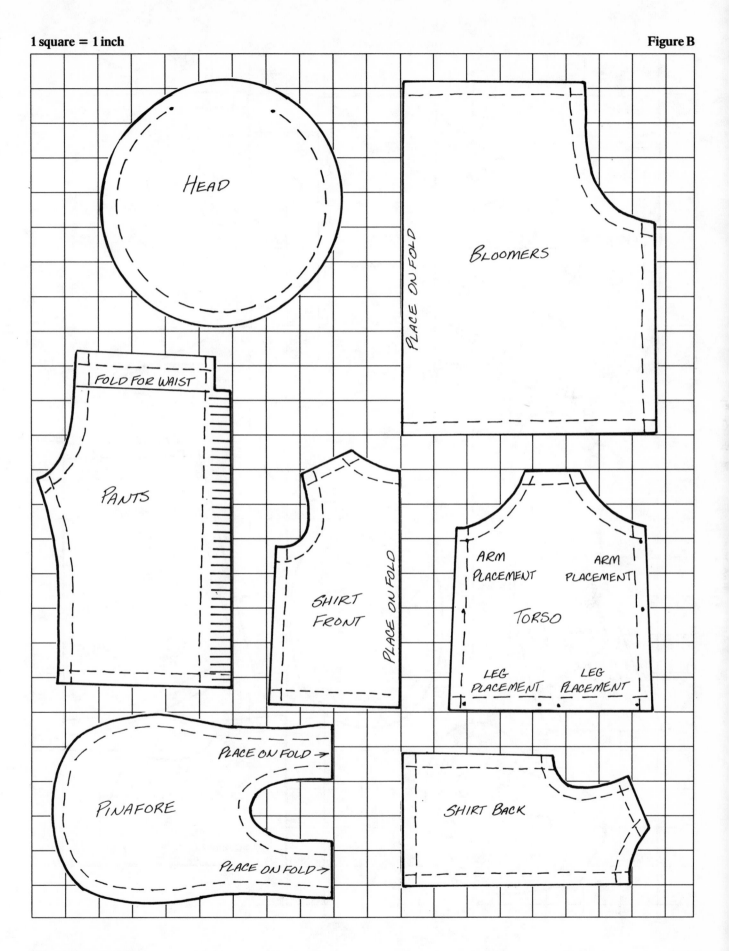

Figure C 1 square = 1 inch

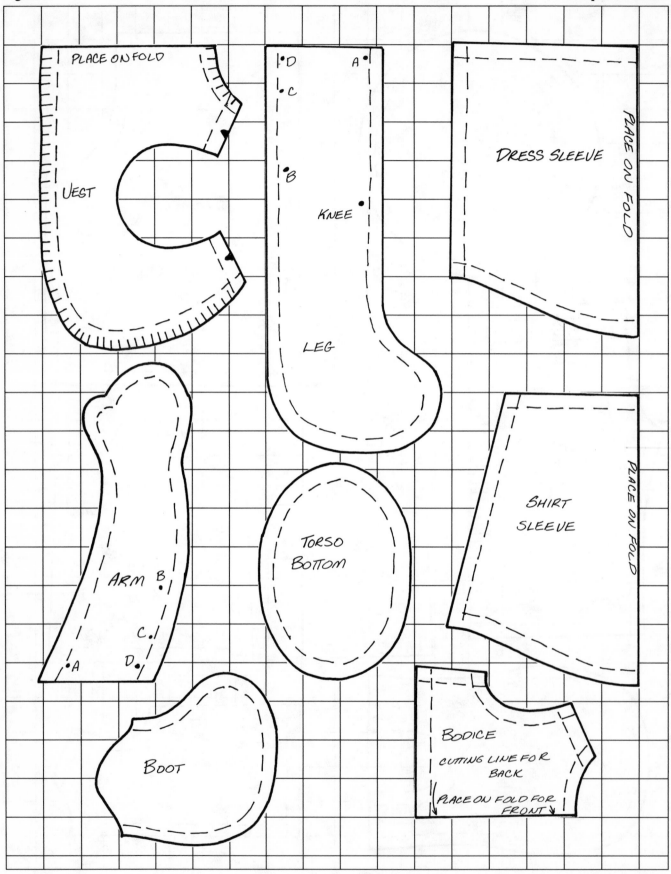

PLACE ON FOLD

VEST

D•
•C

A•

•B

KNEE

LEG

DRESS SLEEVE

PLACE ON FOLD

ARM B•

C•
•A   D•

TORSO
BOTTOM

SHIRT
SLEEVE

PLACE ON FOLD

BOOT

BODICE

CUTTING LINE FOR
BACK

PLACE ON FOLD FOR
FRONT

Arm – cut four
Leg – cut four
Head – cut two
Nose – cut one
Calico:
    Bodice Front – cut one
    Bodice Back – cut two
    Dress Front – cut one, 9 x 13 inches
    Dress Back – cut two, 7 x 9 inches
    Dress Sleeve -cut two
    Shirt Front – cut one
    Shirt Back – cut two
    Shirt Sleeve – cut two
Ivory cotton:
    Bloomers – cut two
    Pinafore – cut one
Fleece:
    Pants – cut four
    Vest – cut one
Brown felt:
    Shoe – cut four
Black felt:
    Boot – cut four

CALLIE

Making the Body

Note: The bodies are identical for both Callie and Caleb. Repeat the instructions for the second doll.

1. To assemble one arm (**Figure D**), place two Arms right sides together and stitch the long contoured seam, beginning at point A and ending at point B. Begin again at C and stitch to D. Leave the seam unstitched between B and C. Leave the short straight edge unstitched. Clip the curves and turn right side out. Press the seam allowances to the inside between B and C. Baste the raw edges together along the open end. Make a second arm in the same manner. Do not stuff the arms just yet.

2. Place two Legs right sides together. Stitch the long contoured seam from point A to point B and then from C to D. Clip the curves and turn right side out. Press the seam allowances to the inside between B and C. Assemble a second leg in the same manner.

3. Place one Torso right side up on a flat surface. Place the arms on top at the arm placement marks (**Figure E**), aligning the basted straight edges along the side edges of the Torso. The arms should be turned so that both thumbs point upward. Baste the arms in place.

4. Place the legs on top of the Torso at the leg placement marks (**Figure E**), aligning the straight edges along the lower edge of the Torso. The toes should point outward. Baste the legs in place.

5. Place the second Torso right side down on top of the stack, sandwiching the arms and legs between (**Figure F**). Stitch the seam from the neck edge to the lower edge on each side, taking care not to catch any of the lower arm or leg fabric in the seams. Leave the neck and lower edges open.

Figure D

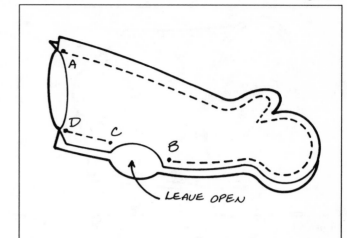

LEAVE OPEN

Figure E

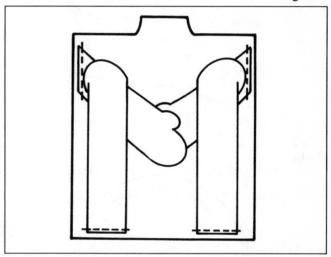

Figure F

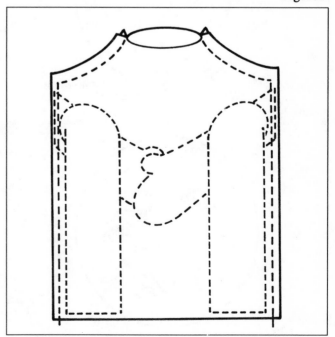

Figure G

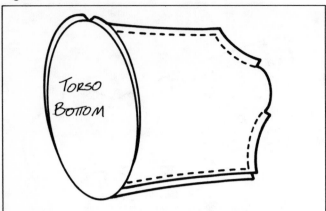

Figure H

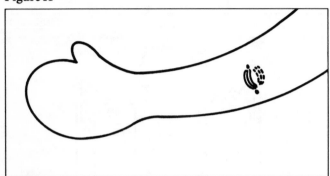

Figure I

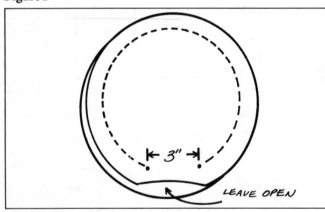

Figure J

6. Leave the torso turned inside out, with the arms and legs sandwiched inside. Pin the Torso Bottom just inside the open lower edge, placing right sides together. Stitch the seam all the way around the edge, easing to fit, as shown in **Figure G**. Clip the curves and corners and turn right side out.

7. Stuff the torso through the neck opening. Stuff the arms and legs through the short openings in the seams and then blindstitch the opening edges together. Press the seam allowance to the inside around the neck edge.

8. To soft-sculpt one elbow, take two or three stitches back and forth through the arm, as shown in **Figure H**. Lock and cut the thread. Repeat for the other arm. To soft-sculpt the knee joints, stitch back and forth through each leg in the same manner. (The knee position is marked on the scale drawing.)

Making the Head

1. Place two Heads right sides together and stitch the seam all the way around the edge, leaving a 3-inch opening, as shown in **Figure I**. Clip the curves and turn right side out. Press the seam allowances to the inside along the opening edges. Stuff the head firmly and blindstitch the opening edges.

2. To form the nose, baste close to the edge all the way around the Nose. Place a small wad of fiberfill in the center and pull the basting threads to gather the fabric tightly around the stuffing. Take a few stitches to secure the gathering.

3. Callie's finished face is shown in **Figure J**. Blindstitch the nose to the approximate center of the face. For the eyes, place one of the black buttons against the face, ¾ to 1 inch from one side of the nose and about ½ inch above it, as shown. Secure by stitching completely through the head several times. Pull the thread so the button is slightly indented. (The indentation on the back of the head will be covered by hair.) Attach the second button in the same manner, on the opposite side of the nose.

4. To work Callie's mouth, use six strands of red embroidery floss and follow the entry and exit points illustrated in **Figure K**. The stitches that go all the way through the head should be pulled to soft-sculpt the face. Stitches that do not go all the way through, but are secured just under the surface of the face, should not be pulled tight.

   a. Knot the floss and insert the needle from the back of the head. Push the needle through the head and exit on the front at point 1, about 1¼ inches below the nose and ½ inch to the left.

   b. Enter at point 2, push the needle through the head and exit on the back of the head opposite point 2.

   c. Reenter at the last exit point and push the needle straight through the head, exiting at point 2 on the front.

   d. Enter at point 3, take a tiny stitch just below the surface and exit just beside point 3.

   e. Enter at point 4, push the needle straight through the head and exit opposite point 4 on the back.

   f. Reenter just beside the last exit point, push the needle through the head and exit at point 4 on the front.

   g. Enter at point 5, push the needle through to the back and exit opposite point 5 on the back.

GREAT FABRIC DOLL BOOK

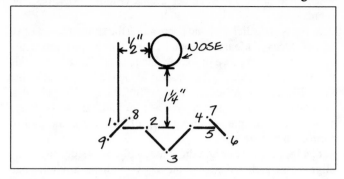

Figure L

h. Reenter just beside the exit point, push the needle straight through to the front and exit at point 6.

i. Enter at point 7, take a long stitch underneath the surface and exit at point 8.

j. Enter at point 9 and push the needle straight through the head to the back. Exit, lock the stitch and cut the thread.

5. To finish the face (**Figure J**), use the black felt-tip marker to draw tiny freckles. To form the eyelashes, draw three short straight lines on the outer side of each eye, as shown. Draw one short straight line above each eye for the eyebrows. Brush cosmetic blusher sparingly across the cheeks and nose.

6. To make Callie's hair (**Figure L**), use about three-fourths of the skein of rug yarn. Cut the yarn into 22-inch lengths. Separate the yarn into groups of five or six strands. Place one bunch across Callie's head, about 1 inch in front of the seam. Stitch it in place at the center point. Continue stitching bunches of yarn to Callie's head in this manner until you have created a continuous center part from the top front to about 2½ inches from the bottom of the head at the back.

7. We tied Callie's hair in pony tails, as shown in **Figure L**. Gather together all of the yarn strands on one side at about eye level and secure it with a spare length of yarn. Glue or tack the hair to Callie's head in several places above the yarn tie to help it stay in place. Make the second pony tail on the opposite side of the head. Cover each yarn tie with an 18-inch length of ivory grosgrain ribbon tied in a bow.

8. To make Callie's center front curl (**Figure L**), use a single strand of yarn and a needle and thread. Begin by stitching one end of the yarn to her forehead at the front of the center part. Do not cut the thread. Wrap the yarn loosely around a pencil or other round object as many times as it will go. Insert the needle between the yarn loops and the pencil. Push it all the way through, pull it out the other end and hold the yarn loops as you remove the pencil. Stitch the curl to Callie's head, securing the loose end of yarn underneath the curl.

9. Place Callie's head on top of her neck with the face pointing upward (the chin should be pointing toward the front of the body). Bend the head downward until the face points forward. Begin at the back and whipstitch around the neck several times to secure the head.

Making the Dress

1. Run a line of basting stitches ½ inch from the upper edge of the Dress Front and pull the thread to gather the edge. Place the Bodice Front and Dress Front right sides together, aligning the lower edge of the Bodice Front with the gathered upper edge of the Dress Front. Adjust the gathers evenly and stitch the seam (**Figure M**). Press the seam allowances toward the bodice.

2. Repeat step 1 to gather and attach one Dress Back to one Bodice Back. Attach the remaining Dress Back to the remaining Bodice Back in the same manner.

3. Place the two dress back assemblies right sides together and stitch the center back seam from the lower edge to about 1¼ inches below the bodice seams. Press the seam open. Press the seam allowances to the wrong side of the dress along the unstitched portion and topstitch in place.

4. Place the dress front and back assemblies right sides to-

Figure N

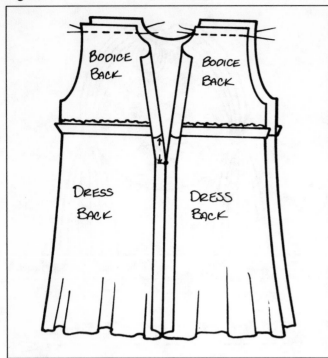

Figure O

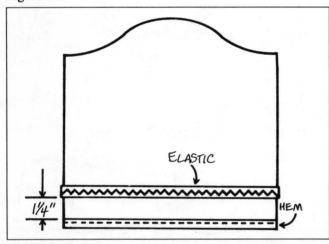

Figure P

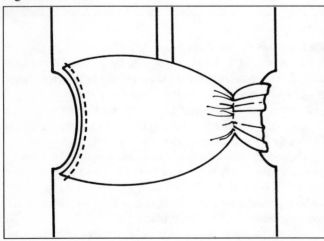

gether and stitch the shoulder seams (**Figure N**). Press the seams open.

5. Press and stitch a ¼-inch hem along the straight lower edge of one Sleeve. Measure around Callie's arm, just above the elbow, and cut a piece of elastic about 1 inch longer than this measurement. Stretch out the elastic along the wrong side of the same Sleeve 1¼ inches from the hemmed edge. Zigzag stitch the elastic in place, stretching it as you go (**Figure O**). Baste ½ inch from the curved upper edge of the Sleeve and pull to form even gathers.

.6. Place the Sleeve and dress assembly right sides together, aligning the gathered edge of the Sleeve with one armhole edge of the dress (**Figure P**). Adjust the gathers to fit and stitch the seam. Press the seam allowances toward the sleeve.

7. Repeat steps 5 and 6 to make and attach a second sleeve.

8. Fold the dress right sides together and stitch the underarm and side seam on each side, as shown in **Figure Q**. Press the seams open.

9. Use a length of binding tape to encase the neck edge of the dress, leaving a 6-inch extension beyond each back corner. The extensions will be used as ties.

10. Double-turn and stitch a narrow hem around the lower edge of the dress.

Bloomers, Pinafore and Shoes

1. Place the two Bloomers right sides together and stitch the center front and back seams (**Figure R**). Clip the curves and press the seams open.

2. Hem the straight lower edge of each bloomer leg. (We used contrasting brown thread, which coordinated with the brown calico we used for the dress.) Measure around Callie's leg, about 3 inches above her ankle. Cut two lengths of elastic, each about 1 inch longer than this measurement. Stretch and stitch one length to the wrong side of each bloomer leg (**Figure S**) 1¾ inches above the hemmed edge, using a zigzag stitch.

3. Fold the bloomers right sides together, matching the center front and back seams, and stitch the inner leg seam, as shown in **Figure T**.

4. To make a casing for the elastic, double-turn and press a ⅜-inch hem to the wrong side of the bloomers around the waist edge. Stitch close to the edge, leaving a short opening in the stitching line. Measure around Callie's waist and cut a piece of elastic about 1 inch longer than this measurement. Thread the elastic through the casing, stitch the ends together and tuck them back into the casing.

5. Encase the entire outer edge of the Pinafore, using the gathered eyelet trim. Encase the neck edge in the same manner (**Figure U**).

6. Dress Callie in her bloomers and dress. Slip the pinafore down over her head. Use the remaining length of ivory grosgrain ribbon as a sash, wrapping it around the pinafore at the waist and tying it in a bow at the back.

7. Place two Shoes right sides together and stitch the seam all the way along the long curved edge (**Figure V**). Clip the curves and turn right side out.

8. Cut the brown grosgrain ribbon into two 10-inch lengths. Stitch the center of one length to the back of one shoe. Place

Meg
page 99

Beth
page 99

Meg & Beth
page 99

Country Gals
page 107

Country Gals
page 107

Baby Grande
page 113

Amos & Agnes Appleknocker
page 117

Changeable Charlene
page 123

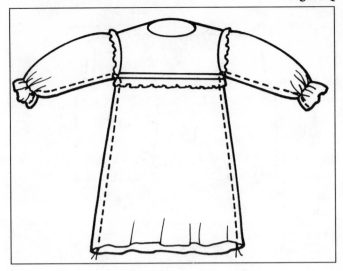

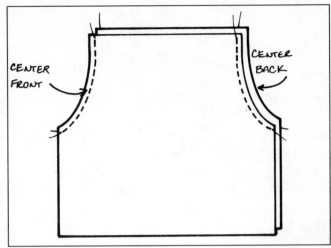

CENTER FRONT

CENTER BACK

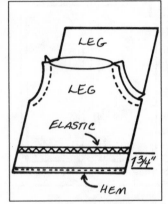

LEG

LEG

ELASTIC

1¾"

HEM

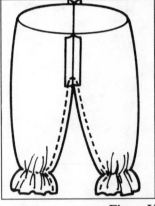

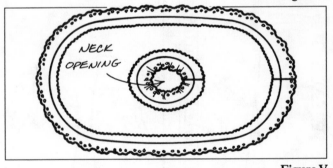

NECK OPENING

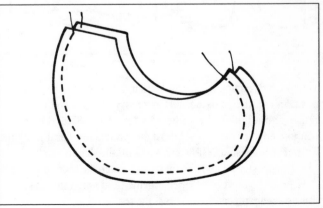

Figure V

the shoe on Callie's foot. Bring the ribbon ends to the front and tie them in a bow. Make a second shoe in the same manner.

CALEB

Caleb is very similar to Callie in several ways. Begin by making Caleb's body, following the same steps and using the same patterns as you did for Callie (see "Making the Body").

Making the Head

Caleb's head is the same as Callie's but his hair is slightly shorter. Follow the instructions for Callie's head, stopping at step 6. Continue with the instructions here for Caleb's hair.

1. Use the remaining rug yarn for Caleb's hair. Cut the yarn into 10-inch lengths and fold each length in half. Place one folded length over Caleb's head with the folded end toward the front, as shown in **Figure W**. The folded end should extend past the head seam about 2 inches. Tack the yarn to Caleb's head near the head seam.

2. Continue tacking folded strands of yarn to Caleb's head in this manner, working along the seam in both directions until you reach a point about even with the top of the mouth on each side. Go back and add additional lengths until you have used all of the yarn or until the hair looks sufficiently thick.

3. Snip a few of the looped front ends of yarn and fold them back over the tacking stitches to hide them. Glue the hair to Caleb's head in a few places.

4. Whipstitch Caleb's head to his body as you did Callie's.

Making the Shirt

1. Place the two Shirt Backs right sides together and stitch the center back seam from the lower edge to about 3½ inches from the neck edge. Press the seam open and press the seam allowances to the wrong side of the shirt along the unstitched portion. Topstitch the pressed seam allowances in place.

2. Place the shirt back assembly and the Shirt Front right sides together and stitch the shoulder seams. Press open.

3. Hem the straight lower edge of one Sleeve. Baste ½ inch

Figure W

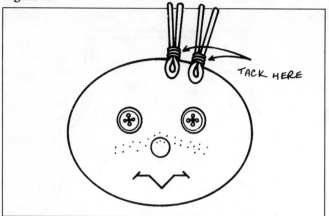

Figure BB

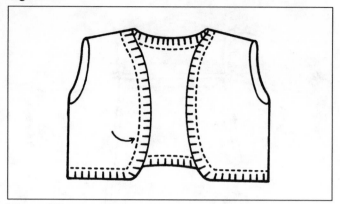

Figure X

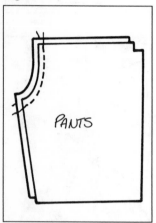

PANTS

Figure Y

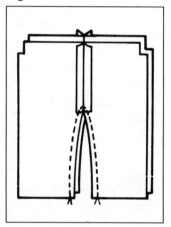

Figure CC

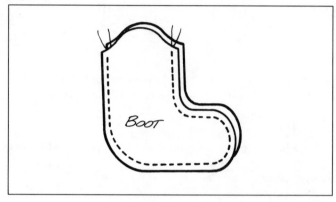

BOOT

Figure Z

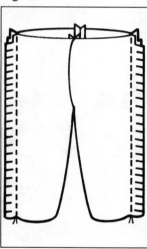

Figure AA

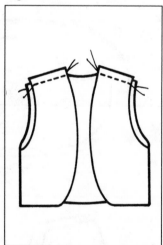

7. Use binding tape to encase the neck edge of the shirt, leaving a 6-inch extension at each center back corner.

8. Hem the lower edge of the shirt.

Pants, Vest and Boots

1. Place two Pants right sides together and stitch the curved center seam, as shown in **Figure X**. Clip the curve and press open. Repeat, using the remaining two Pants.

2. Place the two pants assemblies right sides together and stitch the inner leg seam (**Figure Y**). Press open. Turn each leg inside out so the pants are wrong sides together.

3. To create the chap-style edging (**Figure Z**), stitch a 1-inch-wide seam on each side. (The pants should still be *wrong* sides together.) Clip the seam allowances about ½ inch deep at ¼-inch intervals, as shown.

4. Hem the waist and leg edges of the pants.

5. Place the Vest right side up on a flat surface. Fold the two ends toward the center, aligning the shoulder edges on each side (**Figure AA**). Stitch the shoulder seams, as shown. Press the seams open.

6. Stitch a narrow hem around each armhole opening.

7. To form the fringe, first stay-stitch all the way around the vest, ½ inch from the edge, as shown in **Figure BB**. Make short cuts at about ⅛- or ¼-inch intervals, as shown. Take care that you don't cut through the stay-stitching.

8. Place two Boots right sides together and stitch the seam all the way along the contoured edge, leaving the curved upper edge open (**Figure CC**). Clip the curves and turn right side out. Make a second boot in the same manner.

from the curved upper edge and pull to form even gathers.

4. Pin the Sleeve to the shirt assembly, placing right sides together and aligning the gathered edge of the Sleeve with one armhole edge of the shirt. Adjust the gathers to fit and stitch the seam. Press the seam allowances toward the sleeve.

5. Repeat steps 3 and 4 to make and attach the second sleeve.

6. Fold the shirt right sides together and stitch the underarm and side seam on each side. Press the seams open.

GREAT FABRIC DOLL BOOK

length of ¼-inch white satin ribbon, 1 yard of ¼-inch ecru lace trim and an 8-inch length of 1-inch maroon satin ribbon

Two skeins of brown yarn for the hair

10-inch length of ivory or cream-colored bias edge binding tape

1 yard of ¼-inch-wide elastic

Six ⅜-inch ivory-colored buttons

Two ¾-inch white buttons (We used shank-type buttons in a flower shape.)

Two 2-inch-diameter fabric flowers in a color that coordinates with Beth's dress fabric (We used maroon.)

Dried flowers such as baby's breath for Meg's crown

Florist's wire

Two bags of polyester fiberfill

Embroidery floss in brown, blue, pink and red

Embroidery needle; darning needle (or a needle with eye large enough for yarn)

Regular sewing thread to match the fabrics

Hot-melt glue and a glue gun (or white glue)

Cutting the Pieces

1. Scale drawings are provided in **Figures A** and **B** for the Dress Front/Back, Yoke Front, Yoke Back, Sleeve, Torso, Leg, Shoe, Leg/Foot, Arm and Bloomers. Enlarge the drawings to make full-size paper patterns. (See Tips & Techniques.)

2. Cut the pieces listed in this step from the specified fabric types and colors.

For Meg:

Ivory-colored cotton:
Dress Front – cut one
Dress Back – cut two
Yoke Front – cut one
Yoke Back – cut two
Sleeve – cut two
Bloomers – cut two
Torso – cut two
Arm – cut four
Leg – cut four

Black cotton:
Shoe – cut four

For Beth:

Ivory-colored cotton:
Torso – cut two
Arm – cut four
Leg/Foot – cut four

Maroon cotton:
Dress Front – cut one
Dress Back – cut two
Sleeve – cut two

MEG

Arms, Legs and Torso

Note: All seam allowances are ⅜ inch unless otherwise specified in the instructions.

Meg & Beth

These antique-style dolls bring to mind the romance of yesteryear. They are simple to make, featuring lace-trimmed clothing, embroidered eyes and yarn hair. Meg wears a crown of dried flowers in her hair and Beth has two maroon-colored silk roses. They will be cherished additions to anyone's collection. Each doll is approximately 22 inches tall.

Materials

2½ yards of 45-inch-wide ivory or cream-colored cotton fabric for the doll bodies and for Meg's clothing

½ yard of 36-inch maroon cotton fabric for Beth's dress

8-inch square of black cotton fabric for Meg's shoes

Ivory or cream-colored lace and ribbons for Meg: 1 yard of 2-inch trim, 2 yards of ¼-inch grosgrain ribbon and 2 yards of ½-inch trim

Lace and ribbons for Beth: 2 yards of 3-inch eyelet trim, 12-inch

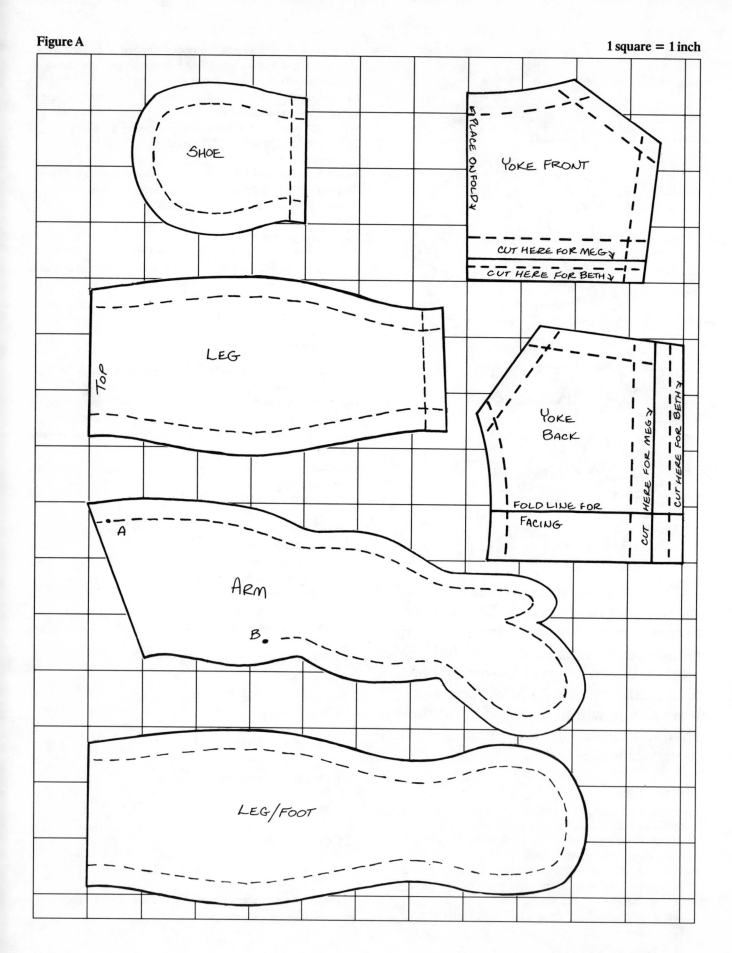

SHOE

YOKE FRONT

← PLACE ON FOLD →

CUT HERE FOR MEG →

CUT HERE FOR BETH →

LEG

TOP

YOKE BACK

CUT HERE FOR MEG →

CUT HERE FOR BETH →

FOLD LINE FOR FACING

A

ARM

B.

LEG/FOOT

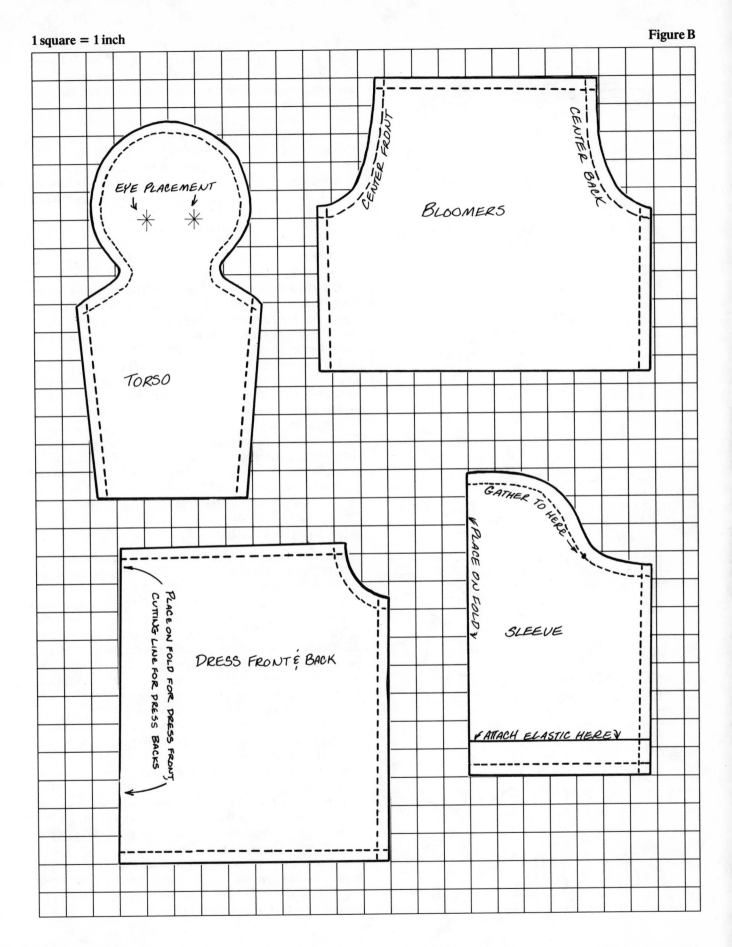

EYE PLACEMENT

TORSO

CENTER FRONT

CENTER BACK

BLOOMERS

DRESS FRONT & BACK

PLACE ON FOLD FOR DRESS FRONT,
CUTTING LINE FOR DRESS BACKS

GATHER TO HERE

PLACE ON FOLD

SLEEVE

ATTACH ELASTIC HERE

Figure C

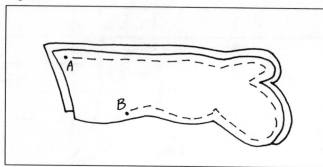

Figure D

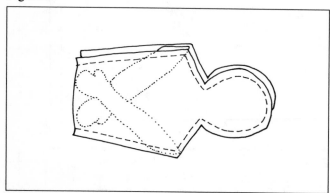

Figure E

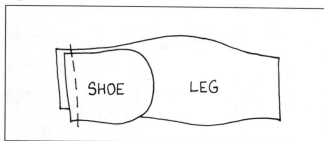

SHOE   LEG

Figure F

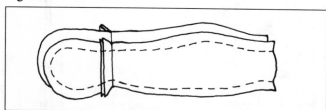

Figure G

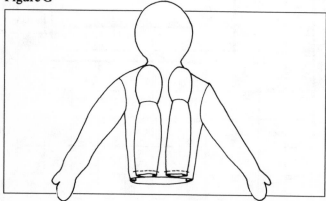

1. Place two Arms right sides together. Begin at point **A** and stitch around the contoured edge to point **B**, as shown in **Figure C**. Clip the curves and turn right side out. Press the seam allowances to the inside between point **B** and the open end. Assemble another arm in the same manner.

2. To assemble the torso (**Figure D**), place one Torso right side up on a flat surface. Pin the arms in place at the tops of the side edges, making sure the thumbs point upward. Pin the second Torso right side down on top of the stack, sandwiching the arms between. Stitch the seam all the way around the contoured edge, leaving the straight lower edge open. (Make sure that you don't stitch any of the lower arm material in this seam.) Clip the curves and corners and turn right side out.

3. Stuff the arms tightly through the seam openings and blindstitch the opening edges together. Stuff the torso and head firmly, leaving ½ inch unstuffed at the bottom.

4. Place a Shoe and Leg right sides together, aligning the straight edge of the Shoe with the short lower end of the Leg. Stitch the seam, as shown in **Figure E**, and press the seam allowances toward the shoe. Repeat to make three more leg-and-shoe assemblies.

5. Place two leg-and-shoe assemblies right sides together and stitch around the contoured edge, leaving the straight top edge open (**Figure F**). Clip the curves, turn right side out and stuff tightly up to ½ inch of the top. Repeat to make a second leg.

6. Place the two legs on top of the torso, as shown in **Figure G**. Stitch across the top of each leg to attach it to the front only. Turn the legs downward and press the seam allowance to the inside around the lower torso edge. Whipstitch together the pressed front and back torso edges.

7. Glue two ⅜-inch buttons to the side of each shoe.

Making the Clothing

1. Turn and press a double ¼-inch hem along the lower edge of each Sleeve. Topstitch ½-inch lace trim to the pressed edge, as shown in **Figure H**.

2. Cut a 5-inch length of elastic. Stretch the elastic across the wrong side of one Sleeve 1 inch from the hemmed lower edge (**Figure I**) and pin the ends in place. (If the elastic won't stretch completely across the fabric, baste across the sleeve width and gather the fabric until it fits the stretched elastic. Adjust the gathers evenly.) Stretch the elastic as you zigzag stitch in place. Do not let the sewing machine needle take any of the pressure or it might break. Repeat for the second Sleeve.

3. Pin the Yoke Front and Yoke Backs right sides together, matching shoulder and armhole edges (**Figure J**). Stitch the shoulder seams and press open.

4. Stitch lace down the center of the Yoke Front, as shown in **Figure K**.

5. Baste along the top of the Dress Front (**Figure L**) and gather evenly to match the width of the Yoke Front. Pin the Dress and Yoke Fronts right sides together, stitch the seam and press the seam allowances toward the dress.

6. Gather the two Dress Backs to match the Yoke Backs in the same manner as you did the Dress Front. Stitch the Dress and Yoke Backs right sides together, matching armhole and back opening edges, as shown in **Figure M**.

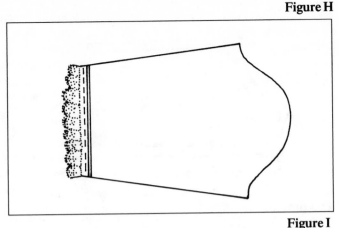

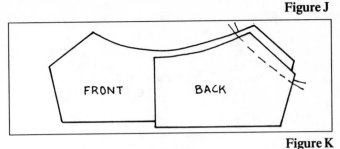

FRONT   BACK

Figure I

Figure K

Figure L

Figure M

YOLK FRONT

YOLK BACK   YOLK BACK

PIN OTHER END OF ELASTIC HERE

7. Place the Dress Backs right sides together (**Figure N**). Stitch the lower portion of the center back seam, leaving the top 6 inches unstitched. Press the seam open.

8. Baste along the curved upper edge of one Sleeve (**Figure O**). Gather the sleeve evenly to fit the armhole opening. Pin the sleeve to the armhole edge, placing right sides together. Stitch the seam and press the allowances toward the sleeve. Attach the second Sleeve in the same manner.

9. Fold the dress right sides together and stitch the underarm and side seams, as shown in **Figure P**. Clip the curves, press the seams open and turn right side out.

10. Hem the lower edge of the dress. Topstitch 2-inch-wide lace to the hemmed lower edge (**Figure Q**), placing the lace so that about ¼ inch extends below the hem. Stitch a length of grosgrain ribbon near the top edge of the lace, as shown.

11. To finish the raw neck edge (**Figure R**), baste a length of ½-inch lace about ¼ inch from the edge. Encase the neck edge in bias tape, making sure the upper edge of the lace is covered by and secured along with the tape.

12. Press under and topstitch the seam allowances along both edges of the back opening, as shown in **Figure S**.

13. **Figure T** shows the finished dress. Cut a 9-inch length of grosgrain ribbon and tie it into a small bow. Tack the bow to the ribbon trim near the bottom of the dress. Tack another ribbon bow to the center front neck edge. Sew two ⅜-inch buttons to the lace along the front yoke.

Making the Bloomers

1. Press under a narrow hem along the lower edge of each Bloomer. Topstitch lace trim to the pressed edge. Stitch elastic

Figure N   **Figure O**

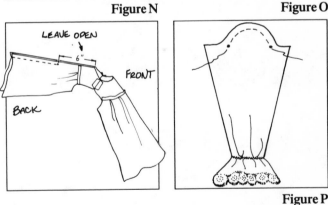

LEAVE OPEN   6"

BACK   FRONT

Figure P

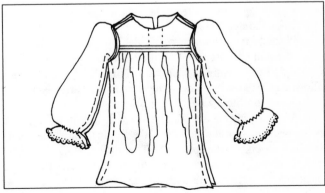

Figure Q

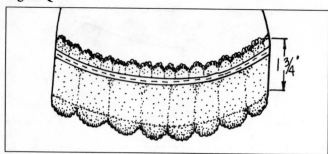

Figure R

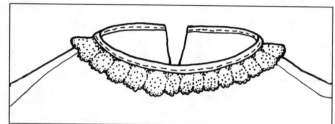

Figure S

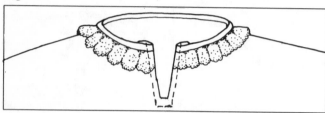

Figure T

Figure U

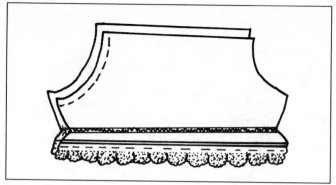

Figure V

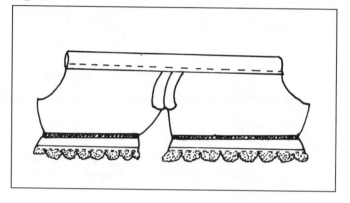

shown in **Figure W**. Clip the curve and press open.

6. Refold the bloomers (still with right sides together), matching the center front and back seams. Stitch the inner leg seam (**Figure X**). Clip the corner and turn right side out.

Making the Hair and Eyes

1. Cut about one hundred 30-inch lengths of yarn. Place the strands across the head and stitch in place along the center part.

2. Pull about twenty lengths to the front for the bangs. These will be trimmed later; for now, use a rubber band or string to hold them out of the way.

3. On each side of the head, tack the yarn in place about where the ear would be (**Figure Y**). Braid the yarn below the tacking stitches and secure the end with a 12-inch-long grosgrain ribbon tied in a bow. Fold the braids back toward the head and tack in place, as shown.

4. To make the star-shaped eyes, thread an embroidery needle with six strands of brown floss. Follow the entry and exit points illustrated in **Figure Z**.

   a. Enter at point 1 on the back of the head underneath the hair (so the knot won't show). Push the needle through the head and exit at 2 on the front.

   b. Pull the floss across the surface and enter at 3. To prevent the floss from showing through the light fabric, take a deep stitch and exit at 4.

   c. Pull the floss across the surface, enter at point 5 and exit at point 6.

   d. Pull the floss across the surface, enter at 7, push the needle through the head and exit at 1 on the back. Lock and cut the floss.

across each leg 2 inches from the hem in the same manner as you did for the sleeves.

2. Place the two Bloomers right sides together (**Figure U**) and stitch the center front seam. Clip the curve and press open.

3. To form a casing at the waist (**Figure V**), press a ¼-inch allowance to the wrong side of the waist edge. Turn again about ½ inch and topstitch close to the pressed edge.

4. Measure and cut a piece of elastic slightly shorter than the doll's waist measurement. Thread the elastic through the casing and tack the ends to the open ends of the casing.

5. Fold the bloomers right sides together and stitch the center back seam, catching the ends of the elastic in the seam, as

Figure X

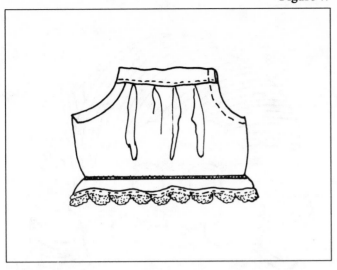

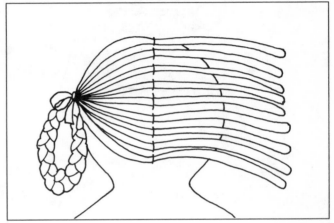

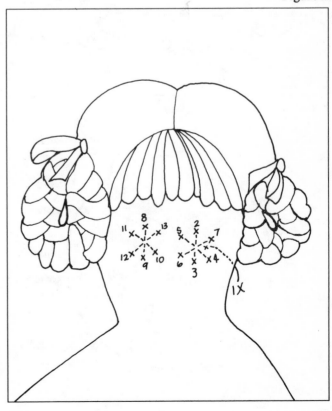

e. Repeat sub-steps a through d to create the other eye, following points 8 through 13.

5. Remove the string holding the yarn bangs and trim them to suit.

6. To make the garland, begin with two or three dried flowers and a length of florist's wire. Stagger the flowers so each blossom is a little below the next, as shown in **Figure AA.** Wrap the wire a few times around the stems. Place the next flower a little lower than the first and wrap the wire around it. Continue adding flowers until the strand is about 12 inches long. Carefully wrap the strand into a circle and secure with wire.

BETH

Arms, Legs and Torso

Assemble the arms, legs and torso in the same manner as you did for Meg, with the following exception: Beth doesn't wear shoes, so skip step 4 in the "Arms, Legs and Torso" section. Use the four Leg/Foot pieces in step 5.

Making the Clothing

1. Assemble the Dress Front, Dress Backs, Yoke Front and Yoke Backs in the same manner as you did for Meg.

2. Beth's dress sleeves are elasticized at the ends rather than above the ends, as Meg's were. Press under a ¼-inch hem along the lower edge of each Sleeve. Turn under another ½ inch and topstitch close to the pressed edge, leaving both ends open.

3. Stitch the sleeves to the dress as you did for Meg. Measure Beth's wrists and cut two lengths of elastic slightly longer. Thread them through the casings and secure the ends.

4. Stitch the underarm and side seams.

5. Figure BB shows the finished dress. Hem the lower edge. Cut a length of 3-inch eyelet trim to fit around the lower edge. Trim it to about 2 inches wide and stitch it to the wrong side of the dress hem, so that it extends below. Topstitch ¼-inch ecru lace to the right side of the dress along the hem. Attach the two ¾-inch buttons to the center of the front yoke, as shown.

6. Cut a 24-inch length of 3-inch eyelet trim for the collar.

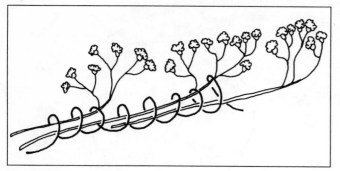

Figure CC

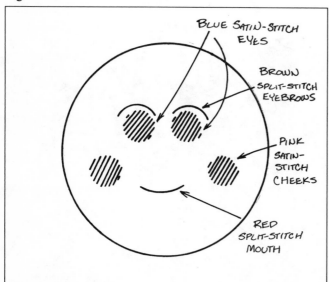

BLUE SATIN-STITCH EYES

BROWN SPLIT-STITCH EYEBROWS

PINK SATIN-STITCH CHEEKS

RED SPLIT-STITCH MOUTH

Fold under and stitch a narrow hem at each end. Fold under the long, bound edge about ½ inch and topstitch ¼ inch from the fold to form a casing. Thread the 12-inch length of ¼-inch white satin ribbon through the casing. Gather the eyelet collar along the ribbon. Wrap the 8-inch length of maroon satin ribbon around Beth's neck, overlap the ends and tack them together. Wrap the eyelet collar around Beth's neck on top of the maroon ribbon. Tie the ribbon ends in a bow at the back.

7. We did not make bloomers for Beth but you may wish to.

Facial Features and Hair

1. We worked satin stitches in blue for the eyes and in pink for the cheeks, as shown in **Figure CC**. Work split stitches in brown floss for the eyelids and in red floss for the mouth line.

2. Beth's hair is made from one pull-skein of brown yarn which has been separated (from the inside out) into four sections. To separate the skein, remove the wrapper, push your fingers into one end, grasp a small portion of yarn and gently pull it out. Do not cut the yarn. Reach inside and pull out two more sections in the same manner. Find a free yarn end, cut a fairly long strand and thread a darning needle with the strand.

3. (Beth does not have ears, but for clarity in steps 3 through 6, when the instructions state "ear" assume that it refers to the spot on her head where the ears would be if she had them.) Stretch out one section of yarn, twist it gently and place it across the top of Beth's head from ear to ear, as shown in **Figure DD**. Tack it in place.

4. Twist another section into a small sphere and tack it in place at ear level. Twist and tack a similar section to the opposite side in the same manner.

5. Place the fourth section across the back of her head, covering the open areas. Tack the yarn in several places to secure it.

6. Tack or glue a silk flower in front of each ear.

24-inch length of ⅛-inch satin ribbon in each of two colors for the neck and bonnet ties (We used pink and beige.)

20-inch length of ½-inch lace trim for the apron

Four ⅜-inch-diameter buttons for the eyes

Thread to match the fabrics

One bag of polyester fiberfill

Two hook-and-eye (or snap) closures

Cutting the Pieces

1. Scale drawings are provided in **Figures A** and **B** for the Body, Dress, Sleeve, Bonnet and Bonnet Brim. Enlarge the drawings to make full-size paper patterns. (Refer to Tips & Techniques, if necessary.)

2. Cut the pieces as listed in this step from the specified types and colors of fabric. (**Note:** If your calico fabric is not wide enough to cut the 4 x 44-inch Apron Tie, cut two 4 x 22½-inch strips and piece them together end to end, as described in Tips & Techniques.)

Muslin:
    Body – cut two for each doll
Dress fabric (quantities are for one dress):
    Dress – cut two
    Sleeve – cut two
    Ruffle Section – cut two, 4 x 27 inches
    Neck Ruffle – cut one, 4 x 17 inches
Calico:
    Apron – cut one, 11 x 18 inches
    Apron Tie – cut one, 4 x 44 inches
    Scarf – cut one, 20 inches square
Second calico:
    Bonnet – cut one
    Bonnet Brim – cut two
    Shawl – cut one, 15 inches square

Making the Body

Note: All seam allowances are ⅜ inch unless otherwise specified in the instructions.

1. Place two Bodies right sides together and stitch around the edge, leaving a 3-inch opening along one side, as shown in **Figure C**. Clip the curves and corners, turn right side out and press the seam allowances to the inside along the opening.

2. Stuff the head fairly full. To define the neck, topstitch across the bottom of the head (**Figure D**). Stuff the legs and topstitch across them where they meet the torso, to define the joints. Stuff the arms and topstitch to define the shoulders. (You do not have to topstitch the neck, leg and shoulder joints, but they will bend more easily if stitched.) Stuff the torso last and whipstitch the opening, as shown.

3. Sew two buttons in place for the eyes. (If the doll is to be made for a young child, the buttons might be a hazard. You may prefer to work embroidered satin stitches or to glue on felt pieces for the eyes.)

4. To make the hair for the doll that wears the scarf (**Figure E**), cut fifty 15-inch lengths of yarn and tie the bunch together at the center. Tack the yarn bunch to the center of the doll's head, as shown. To create the bangs, pull forward about half of the strands on each side. Tirm the bangs. Smooth the remain-

Country Gals

These country girls don't go in for many frills and fancies, preferring muslin and calico. The one-pattern body construction couldn't be simpler – so you might not want to stop with just two dolls. Their clothing is equally simple to sew and is perfectly suited for ribbons and trims of your choice. Let your imagination be your guide. The dolls are about 20 inches tall.

Materials

¾ yard of 36-inch medium-weight unbleached muslin for each doll body

1 yard of 36-inch cotton for each dress (We made one dress from blue polished cotton and one from calico.)

½ yard of calico that coordinates with one of the dress fabrics, for the scarf and apron

½ yard of another calico that coordinates with the other dress fabric, for the bonnet and shawl

One-half skein of brown yarn for each doll's hair

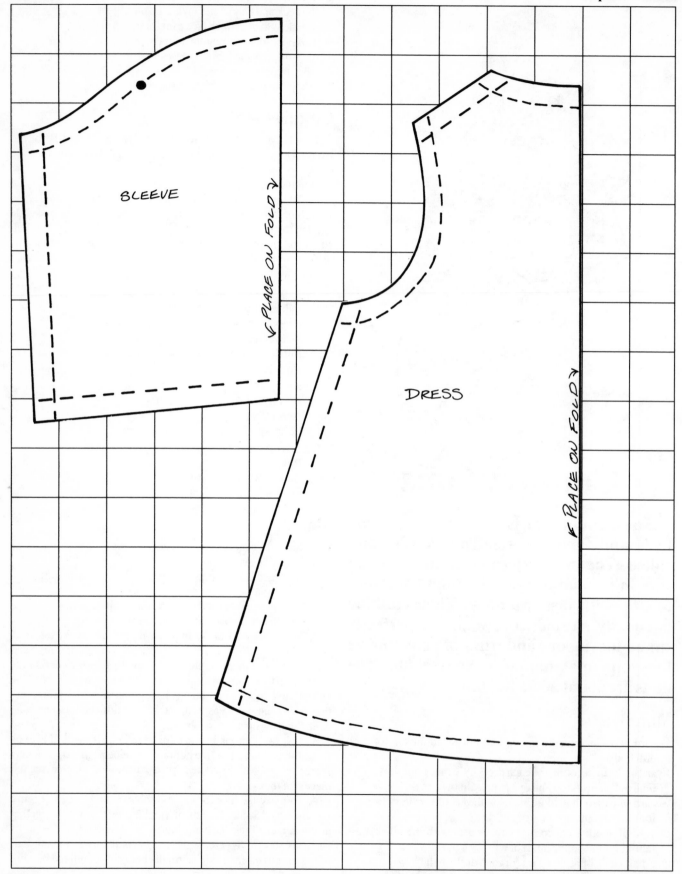

SLEEVE

← PLACE ON FOLD →

DRESS

← PLACE ON FOLD →

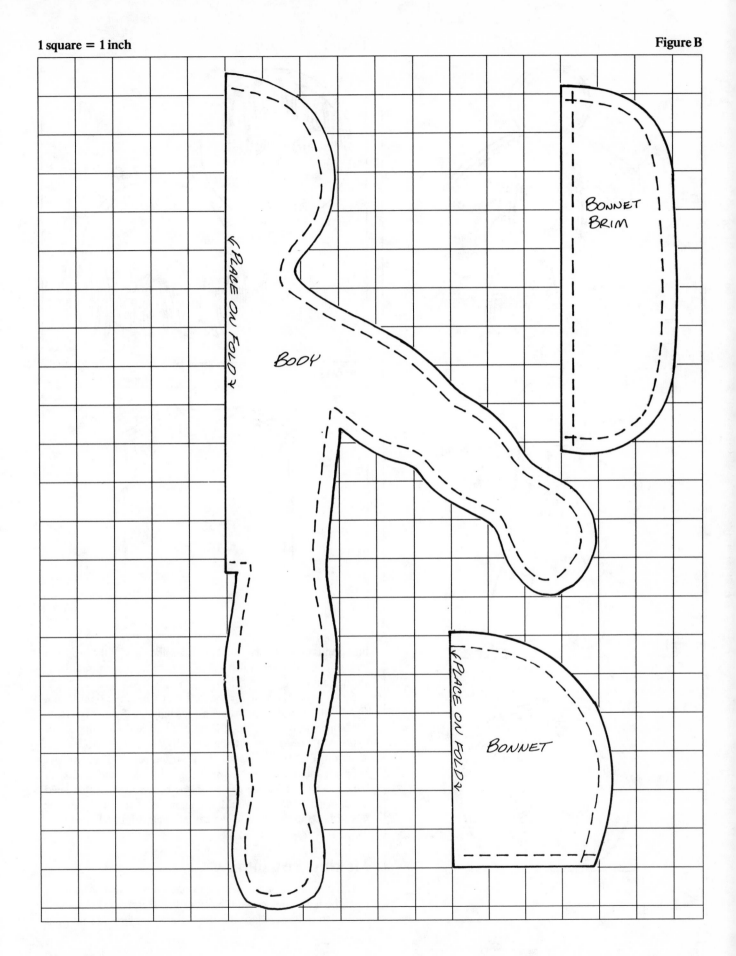

←PLACE ON FOLD→

BODY

BONNET BRIM

←PLACE ON FOLD→

BONNET

Figure C

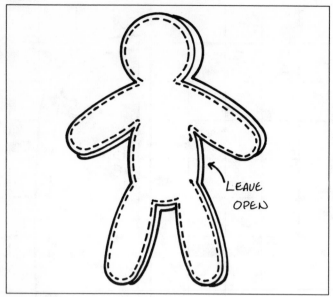

LEAVE OPEN

Figure D

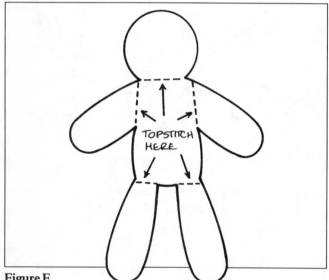

TOPSTITCH HERE

Figure E

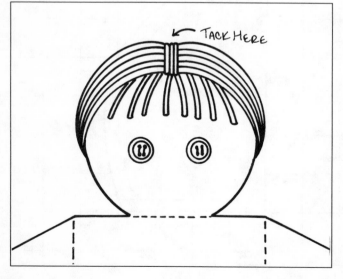

TACK HERE

Figure F

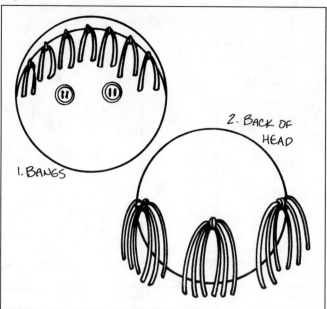

1. BANGS

2. BACK OF HEAD

Figure G

3"

DRESS BACK

ing strands downward around the sides and back of the head and tack or spot glue them just behind where the ears would be if she had any.

5. To make the hair for the doll that wears the bonnet, cut sixty 9-inch lengths and twenty 5-inch lengths of yarn. To create the bangs, fold each 5-inch length in half and tack the center to the doll's head, spacing them evenly along the seam line, as shown in **Figure F**, diagram 1. Trim the bangs, if necessary. Separate the 9-inch lengths into three bunches and fold each bunch in half. Tack the center of one bunch to the doll's head about where one ear would be, another where the other ear would be, and the third to the center back (**Figure F**, diagram 2).

Making the Clothing

1. To create a back opening in one Dress, cut a 3-inch slit from the neck edge down the center line (**Figure G**). This will be the Dress Back. Place the Dress Back and Dress Front right

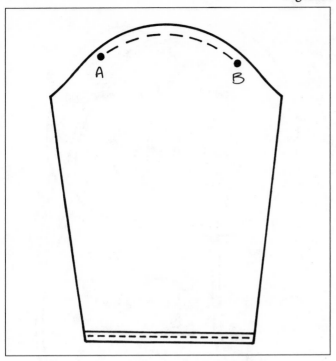

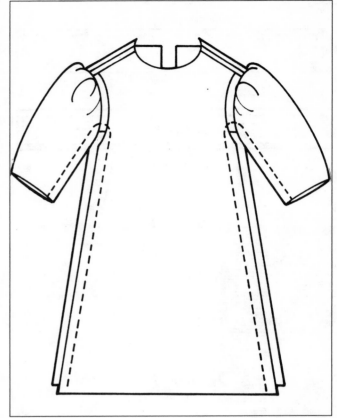

sides together, stitch the shoulder seams and press open.

2. Turn under and stitch a narrow double hem along the straight lower edge of each Sleeve. Baste along the curved upper edge between points **A** and **B**, as shown in **Figure H**, and gather evenly to fit the armhole openings of the dress. Stitch each Sleeve to the dress, placing right sides together and easing the gathers to fit. Press the seam allowances toward the sleeves.

3. Fold the dress right sides together and stitch the underarm and side seams, as shown in **Figure I**. Clip the curves and corners and turn right side out.

4. Piece together the two Ruffle Sections end to end, to form a single 4 x 53-inch strip. Fold the strip in half lengthwise, with right sides together, and stitch across each end. Clip the corners and turn right side out.

5. Pin the ends of the assembled ruffle to the right side of the dress at the center back (**Figure J**), aligning raw edges. Divide and pleat the ruffle evenly around the lower dress edge, forming pleats about 2 inches wide. Stitch in place and turn downward. Press the seam allowances toward the dress.

6. Repeat step 4 to finish the ends of the Neck Ruffle. Repeat step 5 to pleat and stitch the Neck Ruffle to the neck edge of the dress, placing the ends at the back opening corners. Attach a snap or hook-and-eye closure to the neck opening.

7. One doll wears an apron and scarf. Press under a ¼-inch hem along one 18-inch edge of the Apron. Turn under again about 1 inch and stitch. Topstitch ½-inch lace along the hem. Baste ⅜ inch from the opposite 18-inch edge and gather evenly to about 7 inches long. Secure the gathers.

8. Fold the Apron Tie in half lengthwise, placing right sides together. Begin at point **A** and stitch all the way around to point **B**, as shown in **Figure K**, diagram 1. Clip the corners and turn right side out. Press the seam allowances to the inside along the opening. Insert the gathered edge of the apron into the opening.

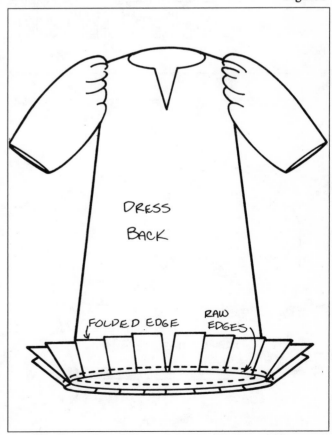

DRESS

BACK

FOLDED EDGE

RAW EDGES

Figure K

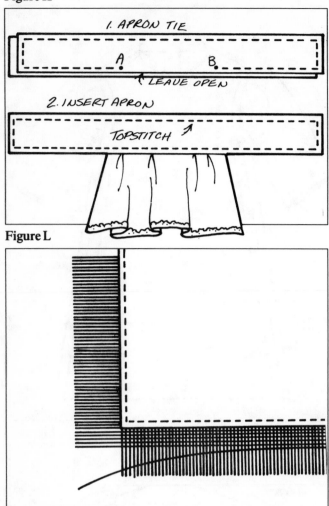

1. APRON TIE

A   B

← LEAVE OPEN

2. INSERT APRON

TOPSTITCH ↗

Figure L

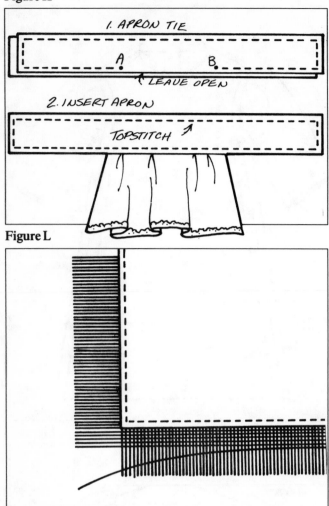

Figure M

BONNET

← BASTE (STEP 12)

BASTE AND GATHER (STEP 11)

Figure N

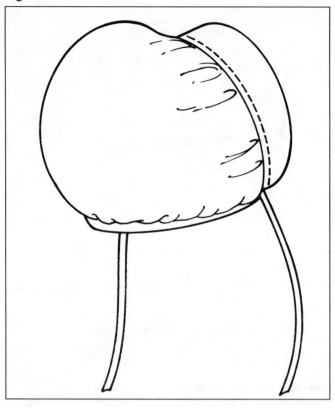

Topstitch completely around the tie to secure the apron (**Figure K**, diagram 2.)

9. You can finish the edges of the Scarf in any manner you like: rickrack, hem, lace or fringe. We created fringe by fraying all four edges. To do this, first stay-stitch around the edges at the desired depth of the fringe (**Figure L**). Pick the first horizontal thread and pull it away from the fabric, as shown. Continue pulling threads on all four sides until it is fringed to suit you. Fold the scarf in half diagonally and wrap it around the doll's head, tying the corners together at the back of the neck. Wrap a length of narrow satin ribbon around the neck ruffle and tie in a bow at the front.

10. The other doll wears a bonnet and shawl. To make the bonnet, place the two Bonnet Brims right sides together and stitch along the curved edge, leaving the straight edge open. Clip the curves and corners, turn right side out and press the seam allowances to the inside along the open edge.

11. Turn under and press a ¼-inch double hem along the long straight edge of the Bonnet, as shown in **Figure M**. Baste close to the hem and gather the edge evenly to about 5½ inches long. Stitch across the gathers to secure them.

12. Baste close to the curved edge and gather evenly to fit the open edge of the brim. Insert the curved edge of the bonnet between the pressed edges of the brim, easing the gathers to fit (**Figure N**). Topstitch to secure. Cut the ⅛-inch satin ribbon in half and tack one length to each corner of the brim, as shown.

13. Finish the edges of the Shawl as you like – we fringed them as we did the scarf. Fold the shawl in half diagonally and wrap it around the doll's shoulders. You can tie the ends together at the front or wrap them underneath her arms.

Baby Grande

You've heard of grandbabies, well, meet Baby Grande. This adorable 25-inch-tall baby doll is soft and cuddly. The sleeper serves as the body, so you don't have to make a separate body and clothing to fit. You can use the sleeper pattern provided, buy one (size 3-6 months) or use a treasured baby sleeper of your own.

Materials

One leg from a pair of regular-weave flesh-tone pantyhose or one nylon stocking, for the head and hands
1 yard of stretchy knit fabric for the body/sleeper (or a purchased sleeper, size 3-6 months)

30-inch length of 2-inch eyelet trim
1½ yards of ⅜-inch satin ribbon
2 yards of white yarn
12-inch length of ¼-inch elastic
One bag of polyester fiberfill
A long sharp needle; flesh-tone heavy-duty thread; and regular thread to match the fabric
Cosmetic cheek blusher
Acrylic paints in white, blue and black; and a fine-tipped artist's paint brush

Cutting the Pieces

1. A scale drawing is provided in **Figure A** for the Body. Enlarge the drawing to make a full-size paper pattern. (See Tips & Techniques.)
2. Cut from knit fabric two Bodies, using the pattern; and one Bonnet, 6 x 20 inches.

Making the Head

1. Tie a knot at the top of the leg of hose (**Figure B**). Measure 10 inches down from the knot and cut across the hose. Turn the hose so the knot is on the inside.
2. Stuff the hose to form a head about 17 inches in circumference (**Figure C**). Tie the hose in a knot at the neck.
3. Soft-sculpt the facial features, using a long sharp needle and flesh-tone heavy-duty thread and following the entry and exit points illustrated in **Figure D**.

    a. Enter at 1, push the needle through the head and exit at point 2.

    b. To form the nose, sew a circle of tiny running stitches about 2 inches in diameter, exiting at 2. Use the tip of the needle carefully to lift fiberfill within the circle and pull the thread until a small round nose appears. Lock the stitch under the bridge of the nose and exit at 2.

    c. To form the nostrils, reenter at 2 and exit at 4.

    d. Enter ¼ inch above 4 and exit at 3. Reenter at 3 and exit at point 5.

    e. Enter ¼ inch above 5 and exit at 2. Lock the stitch at point 2.

    f. To form the eyes, reenter at 2 and exit at 6.

    g. Sew a curved line of small running stitches around to 7. Lift fiberfill within the curved area and lock the stitch at point 7.

    h. Pull the thread across the surface, enter at 8 and exit at point 2.

    i. Pull the thread across the surface, enter at 7 and exit at 2. Lock the stitch at 2. Reenter at 2 and exit at 3.

    j. Repeat sub-steps f through i to sculpt the other eye, using points 3, 9, 10 and 11. Lock the stitch at 3.

    k. To form the mouth, reenter at 3 and exit at 12. Pull the thread across the surface, enter at 13 and exit at 2. Pull the thread until the smile appears. Lock the stitch at 2.

    l. To form the bottom lip, reenter at 2 and exit at 14. Pull the thread across the surface, enter at 15 and exit at 3. Pull the thread until the bottom lip appears. Lock the stitch at 3 and cut the thread.

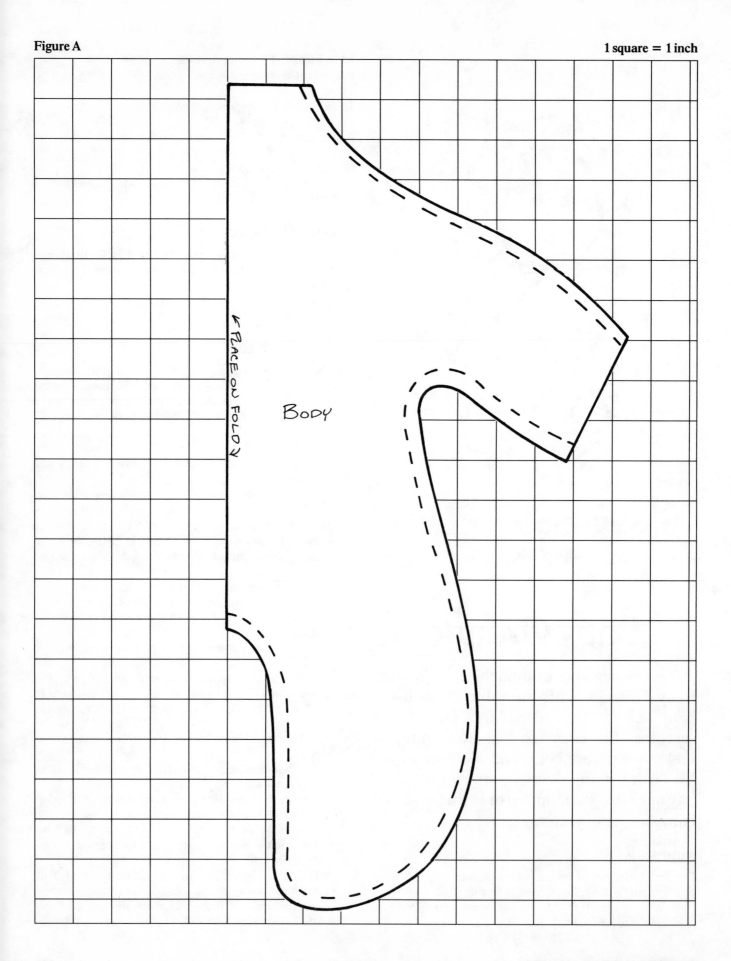

PLACE ON FOLD

Body

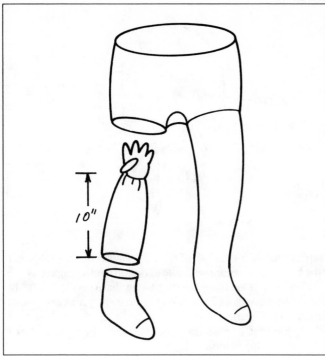

Figure C

Figure E

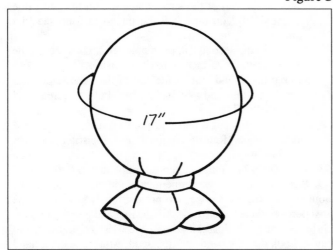

Figure F

4. The finished face is shown in **Figure E**. Paint each eye socket white and let the paint dry. Paint a blue iris in the center, let the paint dry and then add a small black pupil in the center of each iris. Brush cosmetic blusher across the cheeks and bottom lip and dab a little on the nose.

Assembling the Body

Note: If you are using a ready-made sleeper, skip steps 1 and 5 and proceed with steps 2 through 4.

1. Place the two Bodies right sides together and stitch the seams, leaving the wrist and neck edges open (**Figure F**). Clip the curves and corners and turn right side out.

2. Work through the neck opening to stuff the entire body until it is plump but not hard.

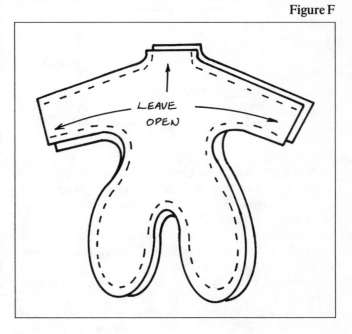

Figure G

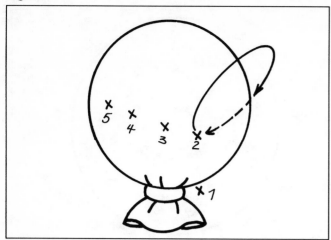

Figure H

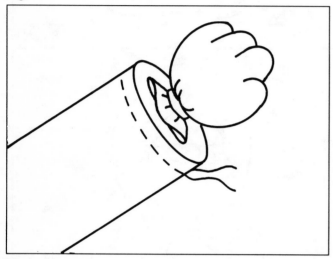

Figure I

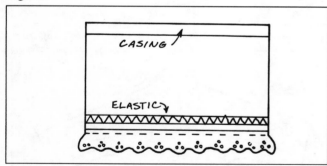

CASING

ELASTIC

Figure J

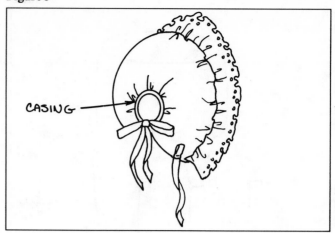

CASING

wrap it around a 3-inch ball of fiberfill. Gather the hose together at the bottom and secure with thread tied around it (**Figure G**).

7. Soft-sculpt the fingers, using a long sharp needle and flesh-tone heavy-duty thread and following the entry and exit points illustrated in **Figure G**.

   a. Enter at 1, push the needle through the hand and exit at 2 on top of the hand.

   b. Slightly flatten the ball of fiberfill. Wrap the thread around the end of the hand, enter at 2 on the palm side and exit at 2 on top. Pull the thread to form the first finger. Lock the stitch at 2.

   c. To form the second finger, reenter at 2, push the needle underneath the surface and exit at 3 on top.

   d. Wrap the thread around the end of the hand, enter at 3 on the bottom and exit at 3 on top. Pull the thread and lock the stitch.

   e. Repeat sub-steps c and d at points 4 and 5 to form the other fingers. Return to point 1, lock the stitch and then cut the thread.

8. Repeat step 7 to sculpt fingers on the other hand.

9. Baste around one wrist opening of the body (**Figure H**), about ¼ inch from the edge. Do not cut the thread. Insert the wrist portion of the hand inside the opening and gather the body fabric around it. Whipstitch around the wrist several times to secure. Lock the stitch and cut the thread. Attach the other hand in the same manner.

10. Tie lengths of white yarn around the Baby Grande's wrists and ankles.

Making the Bonnet

1. Turn under and stitch a narrow hem along one long edge of the Bonnet. Stitch eyelet trim along the hemmed edge. Stretch out the elastic along the wrong side of the fabric, ¾ inch from the hemmed edge. Zigzag stitch the elastic in place, stretching it as you go (**Figure I**).

2. Press under a ¼-inch hem along the opposite long edge. To form a casing, turn it under again about ½ inch and stitch. Thread an 18-inch length of ribbon through the casing. Gather the casing tightly along the ribbon and tie the ends in a bow (**Figure J**). Tack an 18-inch length of ribbon to each lower corner, as shown, and tie the ribbons under baby's chin.

3. Turn under and stitch a narrow hem around the neck edge. Baste about ¼ inch from the hemmed edge and gather evenly until the neck opening measures approximately 2 inches in diameter. Secure the gathers.

4. Center the head over the neck opening, inserting the neck knot inside the body. Begin at the back and whipstitch around the neck several times to secure the head.

5. Turn under and stitch a ¼-inch-wide hem around each wrist opening.

6. To make one hand, cut a 4-inch circle of pantyhose and

Amos & Agnes Appleknocker

What a pair! Amos and Agnes are our answer to the sad lack of elderly members in the doll world. With so many modern families spread out across the country, this couple will provide a sweet reminder of Grandma and Grandpa to the little ones. They are over 3 feet tall.

Materials

Two pairs of regular-weave flesh-tone pantyhose or four nylon stockings, for the heads and hands

1½ yards of 45-inch flesh-tone single-knit polyester for the doll bodies

1½ yards of 45-inch cotton print fabric for the dress

1½ yards of 45-inch denim for the overalls

Two 9 x 45-inch pieces of corduroy, one blue and one black, for the shoes

One size 5 long sleeve boy's shirt

2 yards of 2-inch gathered eyelet trim

9-inch length of 1½-inch flat lace

12-inch length of 1-inch-wide seam binding

18-inch length of ¼-inch elastic

Two metal buckles without prongs, about 2 x 2 inches, for the overall straps

One ¾-inch-diameter button

Five pounds of polyester fiberfill

Long sharp needle; heavy-duty flesh-tone thread; and regular thread to match the fabrics

Hot-melt glue and a glue gun (or white glue)

Cosmetic cheek blusher

Acrylic paints in red, blue, black and white; and a fine-tipped paint brush

Cutting the Pieces

Note: Because the body size will vary depending upon the amount of stuffing, we suggest that you assemble the bodies before cutting the pieces for the clothing. Compare the enlarged clothing patterns to the dolls and adjust them if necessary.

1. Scale drawings are provided in **Figure A** for the Overalls, Shoe, Bodice Front and Bodice Back. Enlarge the drawings to make full-size paper patterns. (See Tips & Techniques.)

2. Cut the pieces listed in this step from the specified fabric types and colors.

Single knit (for *each* doll):
  Torso – cut two, 12 x 15 inches
  Arm – cut two, 8 x 14 inches
  Leg – cut two, 8 x 17 inches
Cotton print:
  Bodice Front – cut one
  Bodice Back – cut two
  Sleeve – cut two, 14 x 20 inches
  Skirt – cut one, 24 x 45 inches
Denim:
  Overalls – cut two
  Bib – cut one, 6½ x 8½ inches
  Strap – cut two, 5 x 15 inches
Blue corduroy:
  Shoe – cut four
Black corduroy:
  Shoe – cut four

Making the Bodies

1. Place two Torsos right sides together and stitch the seams (**Figure B**), leaving a 4-inch neck opening and 3-inch armhole openings. Leave the lower edge open as well. Clip the corners, turn right side out and press the seam allowances to the inside along the neck and arm openings. Stuff firmly.

OVERALLS

← PLACE ON FOLD →

BODICE BACK

BODICE FRONT

← PLACE ON FOLD →

SHOE

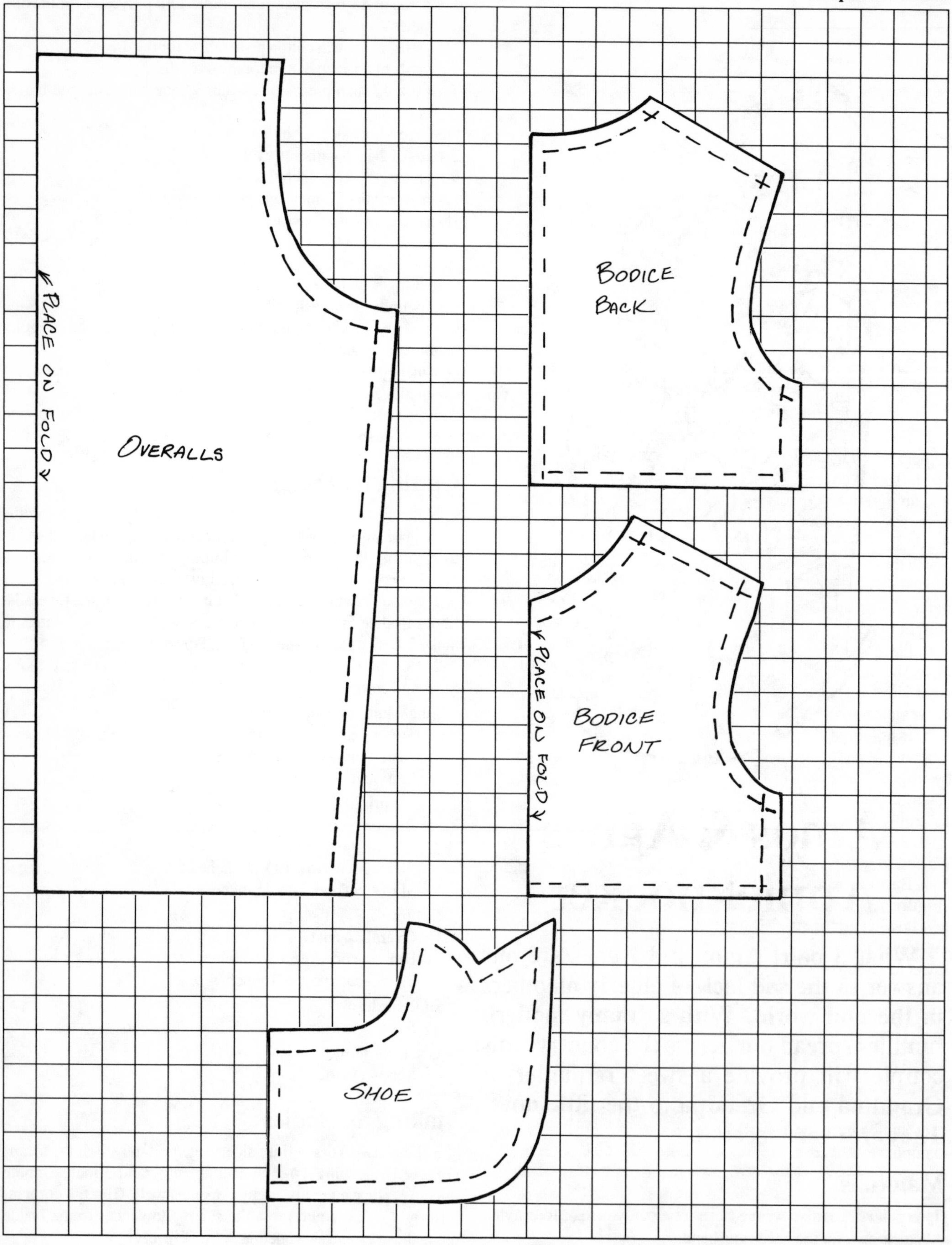

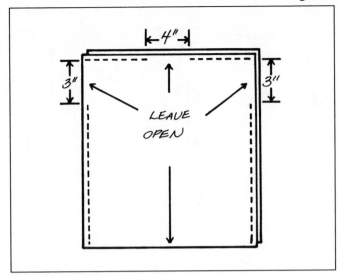

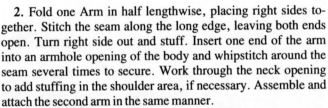

Figure C

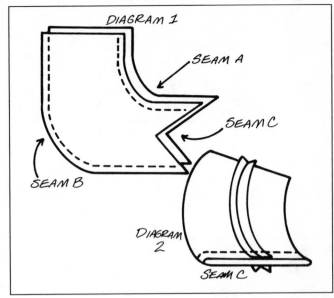

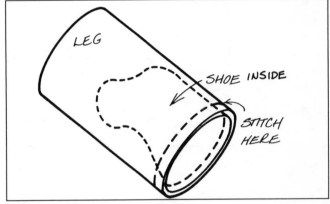

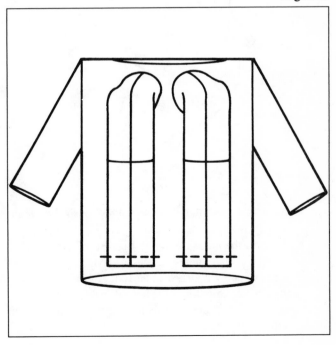

2. Fold one Arm in half lengthwise, placing right sides together. Stitch the seam along the long edge, leaving both ends open. Turn right side out and stuff. Insert one end of the arm into an armhole opening of the body and whipstitch around the seam several times to secure. Work through the neck opening to add stuffing in the shoulder area, if necessary. Assemble and attach the second arm in the same manner.

3. Fold one Leg in half lengthwise, placing right sides together. Stitch the long seam, leaving both ends open. Do not stuff or turn yet.

4. Place two Shoes right sides together and stitch seams **A** and **B**, as shown in **Figure C**, diagram 1. Refold the shoe, still with right sides together, and stitch seam **C** (diagram 2). Clip the curves and corners and turn right side out.

5. Insert the shoe inside the leg (**Figure D**), aligning the ankle edge of the shoe with one end of the leg. The leg seam should be aligned with the center back shoe seam. Stitch the ankle seam, clip the curves and pull the shoe out of the leg. Turn the assembly right side out and stuff firmly.

6. Repeat steps 3 through 5 to assemble and stuff a second leg and shoe.

7. Baste the tops of the legs to the lower edge of the front torso (**Figure E**), with the toes pointing toward the torso. Turn the legs downward and turn the seam allowance to the inside around the lower torso edge. Whipstitch together the front and back lower torso edges.

8. Repeat this section to make a second body.

Adding the Heads and Hands

1. To form a head, tie a knot at the top of a leg of hose. If you are using pantyhose, cut 1 inch above the knot to separate the leg from the panty. Cut across the leg 10 inches below the knot and turn the hose so the knot is on the inside. Stuff and manipulate to form a head approximately 20 inches in circumference (**Figure F**). Tie the hose in a knot at the neck.

2. To soft-sculpt Agnes' facial features, use a long sharp needle and flesh-tone heavy-duty thread and follow the entry and exit points illustrated in **Figure G**.

Figure F

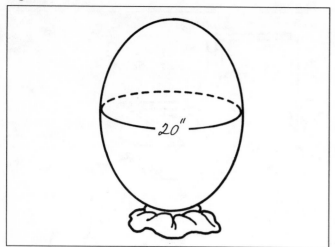

Figure G

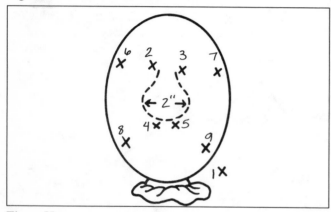

Figure H

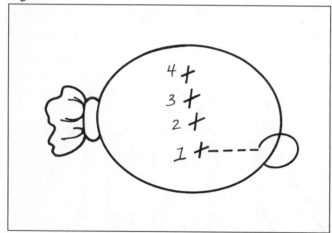

a. Enter at 1, just above the neck knot, push the needle through the head and exit at 2.

b. To form the nose, reenter at 2 and sew a pear-shaped outline of small running stitches, making the lower end approximately 2 inches wide. Exit at 3. Use the tip of the needle carefully to lift fiberfill within the outlined area. Pull the thread to define the nose and lock the stitch between 2 and 3.

Figure I

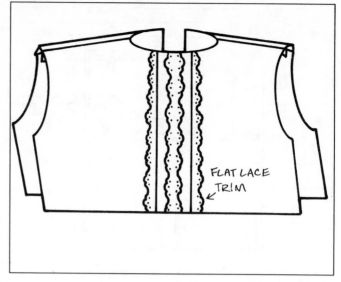

FLAT LACE TRIM

c. To form the nostrils, reenter at 2 and exit at 4. Enter ¼ inch above 4 and exit at 3.

d. Reenter at 3 and exit at 5. Enter ¼ inch above 5 and exit at 2. Lock the stitch at 2.

e. To form the eyes, reenter at 2 and exit at 6. Pull the thread across the surface, enter at 2 and exit at 3.

f. Reenter at 3 and exit at 7. Pull the thread across the surface, enter at 3 and exit at 2. Gently pull the thread until the eye lines appear and lock the stitch at 2.

g. To form the mouth, reenter at 2 and exit at 8.

h. Pull the thread across the surface, enter at 9 and exit at 3. Gently pull the thread until a smile forms and lock the stitch at 3.

i. Reenter at 3 and exit at 1. Lock and cut the thread.

3. Soft-sculpt facial features on Amos' head in the same manner, making his nose a bit larger. Painted details and hair will be added later.

4. To make one hand, cut an 8-inch circle of hose and wrap it around a fist-sized ball of fiberfill. Gather the hose and secure with thread, as shown in **Figure H**. Make three more hands in the same manner.

5. To soft-sculpt the fingers on each hand, follow the entry and exit points illustrated in **Figure H**.

a. Enter at 1 on the palm and push the needle through the hand, exiting at 1 on top.

b. Stitch up and down through the hand to the end. Push the needle through the hand and exit at 1 on the palm. Pull the thread firmly to separate the thumb and lock the stitch at 1.

c. Reenter at 1 and exit at 2 on top.

d. Repeat sub-steps b and c at points 2 through 4 to form the other fingers. Lock the stitch and cut the thread.

6. To attach the head to the body, baste around the neck opening about ¼ inch from the edge. Gather to about 2 inches across. Insert the neck knot inside the opening, making sure the face points in the same direction as the toes. Whipstitch around the neck several times.

7. To attach one hand, baste about ¼ inch from the open wrist

Figure J

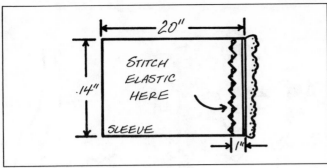

Figure K

Figure L

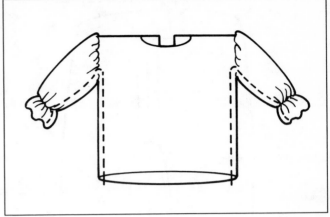

Figure M

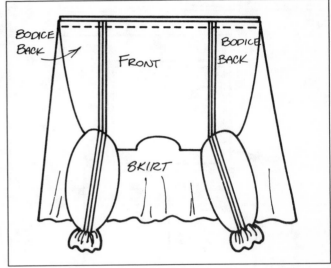

Figure N

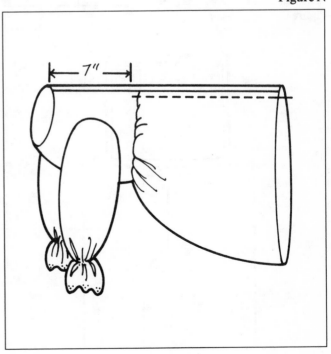

end of the arm. Insert the wrist portion of the hand and gather the arm to fit. Whipstitch around the wrist to secure. Attach each hand in this manner.

Making Agnes' Dress

Note: Seams are ⅜ inch unless otherwise specified.

1. Place the Bodice Front and Backs right sides together. Stitch the shoulder seams and press open. Topstitch flat lace down the center of the Bodice Front (**Figure I**).

2. Turn under and stitch a ¼-inch hem along a 14-inch edge of one Sleeve. Topstitch eyelet trim along this edge. Stretch a 9-inch length of elastic across the wrong side, about 1 inch from the hemmed edge (**Figure J**), and zigzag stitch.

3. Baste along the opposite 14-inch edge and gather evenly to fit the armhole edge of the bodice assembly. Pin the Sleeve and bodice right sides together and stitch the seam (**Figure K**). Clip the curve and press the seam allowances toward the sleeve.

4. Repeat steps 2 and 3 to assemble the second sleeve.

5. Fold the bodice right sides together and stitch the underarm and side seams, as shown in **Figure L**. Clip the corners and press open.

6. Baste along one 45-inch edge of the Skirt. Gather evenly to fit the lower edge of the bodice, as shown in **Figure M**. Pin the bodice and Skirt right sides together and stitch the waist seam. Press the seam allowances toward the skirt.

7. Fold the dress right sides together and stitch the center back seam (**Figure N**), leaving a 7-inch opening at the top. Press the seam open. Press the seam allowances to the wrong side along the open portion and topstitch in place.

8. Fold under and press the seam allowance around the neck edge. Topstitch eyelet trim around the neckline.

Figure O

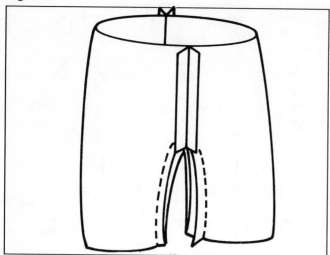

Figure P

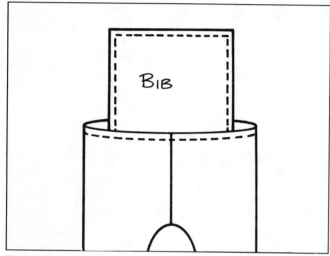

BIB

Figure Q

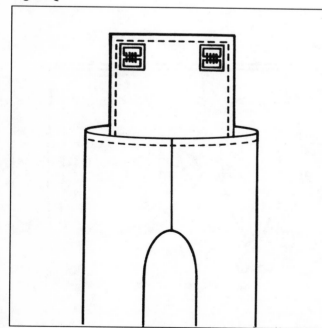

Figure R

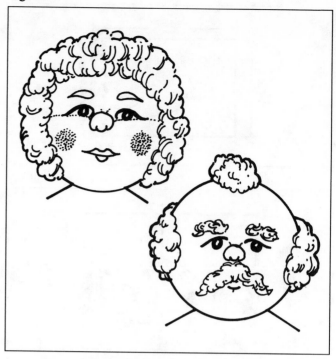

9. Sew the button to one back corner of the neck opening. Work a buttonhole in the opposite corner.

Making Amos' Overalls

1. Place the two Overalls right sides together and stitch the curved center front and back seams. Clip the curves and press.

2. With right sides still together, align the center front and back seams and stitch the inner leg seam (**Figure O**). Clip the curves, press open and turn right side out. Press the waistline seam allowance to the inside.

3. Turn under and topstitch all four edges of the Bib. Center one long edge underneath the front waistline of the overalls and topstitch all the way around the waist (**Figure P**).

4. Fold one Strap in half lengthwise, placing right sides together. Stitch the long seam, leaving both ends open. Turn right side out and press. Stitch a second strap in the same manner.

5. Pin one end of each strap underneath the waistline at the back of the overalls, placing them about 1¼ inches from each side of the center back seam. Topstitch in place.

6. Stitch a buckle to each upper corner of the bib (**Figure Q**).

7. Dress Amos in his overalls. If the waist is too large, zigzag stitch a length of elastic across the back waistline to make it fit Amos' plumply stuffed physique. Hem the overalls legs to fit.

Finishing

The finished faces are shown in **Figure R**. Paint the eye sockets white, allow to dry and paint a blue iris in the center of each eye. Add black pupils and black outlines, as shown. To create Agnes' eyebrows, paint thick white lines above the eyes. Paint her lips red. To create Amos' eyebrows and mustache, glue tufts of fiberfill in place. Glue fiberfill to the heads, as shown, for the hair. Brush cosmetic blusher across their cheeks.

Changeable Charlene

Charlene is a 24-inch-tall quick-change artist whose felt facial features are attached by nylon fastener strips. She keeps extra eyes, eyebrows and mouths in her shoulder bag. Charlene is also a teaching toy, who can help youngsters learn to zip, button and tie.

Materials

1 yard of cotton print for the torso, legs and skirt
½ yard of pink cotton fabric for the shirt and shoes
½ yard of flesh-tone fleece for the head, ears and hands
9½ x 13-inch piece of pink felt for the purse
6 x 8-inch piece of fusible interfacing
Felt scraps in white, blue, black, red and pink for the features
1¾ yards of ⅜-inch white satin ribbon
12-inch length of ½-inch lace trim
6-inch length of ¾-inch lace trim
14-inch length of ¼-inch elastic for the skirt
One skein of yellow yarn for the hair
One ¾-inch button for the purse
One 7-inch skirt zipper for the purse
One bag of polyester fiberfill
Small nylon fastener spots or strips for the facial features
Long sharp needle; heavy-duty flesh-tone thread; and regular thread to match the fabrics
Hot-melt glue and a glue gun (or white glue)

Cutting the Pieces

1. Full-size patterns are provided in **Figure A** for the facial features. Trace the patterns.

2. Scale drawings are provided in **Figure B** for the Hand, Ear, Purse, Torso, Sleeve/Leg, Shoe, Shirt Applique and Head. Enlarge the drawings to make full-size patterns. (Refer to Tips & Techniques, if necessary.)

3. Cut the pieces listed in this step from the specified fabrics. The changeable facial features will be cut later.

Cotton print:
    Torso – cut two
    Leg – cut two
    Skirt – cut one, 11 x 40 inches

Pink cotton:
    Sleeve – cut four
    Shirt Applique – cut one
    Shoe – cut four

Pink felt:
    Purse – cut one
    Purse Strap – cut one, 1 x 13 inches

Fleece:
    Head – cut two
    Ear – cut four
    Hand – cut four
    Nose – cut one, 2-inch-diameter circle

Fusible interfacing:
    Shirt Applique – cut one

Making the Body

Charlene's clothing also serves as her body, so you don't have to make a body and separate clothing to fit. Her shirt front is appliqued to the front torso to give the illusion of an actual shirt. **Note:** All seam allowances are ½ inch unless otherwise specified in the instructions.

1. Place one Torso right side up on a flat surface. Place the fusible Shirt Applique on top, aligning the shoulder edges, and place the fabric Shirt Applique right side up on top. (Placement lines for the applique are provided on the Torso pattern.) Trim away any excess fusible material. Follow the manufacturer's instructions to fuse the pieces together.

2. Zigzag stitch over the side and lower edges of the applique to secure it, as shown in **Figure C**. (If you prefer, this can be done by hand, using a closely spaced blanket stitch.) Stitch ¾-inch lace trim down the center front of the applique. Stitch ½-inch lace trim around the perimeter of the applique to hide the zigzag stitches.

3. Place two Sleeves right sides together and stitch the long side seams (**Figure D**), leaving both ends open. Clip the curves, press the seams open and turn right side out. Hem the larger open end. Make a second sleeve in the same manner.

4. Fold one Leg right sides together and stitch the long side seam, leaving both ends open. Clip the curves, press open and turn right side out. Hem the larger open end. Make a second leg in the same manner.

5. Place the two Torsos right sides together and stitch around the outer edges (**Figure E**), leaving the neck open and leaving

EYES

EYE BROWS

MOUTHS

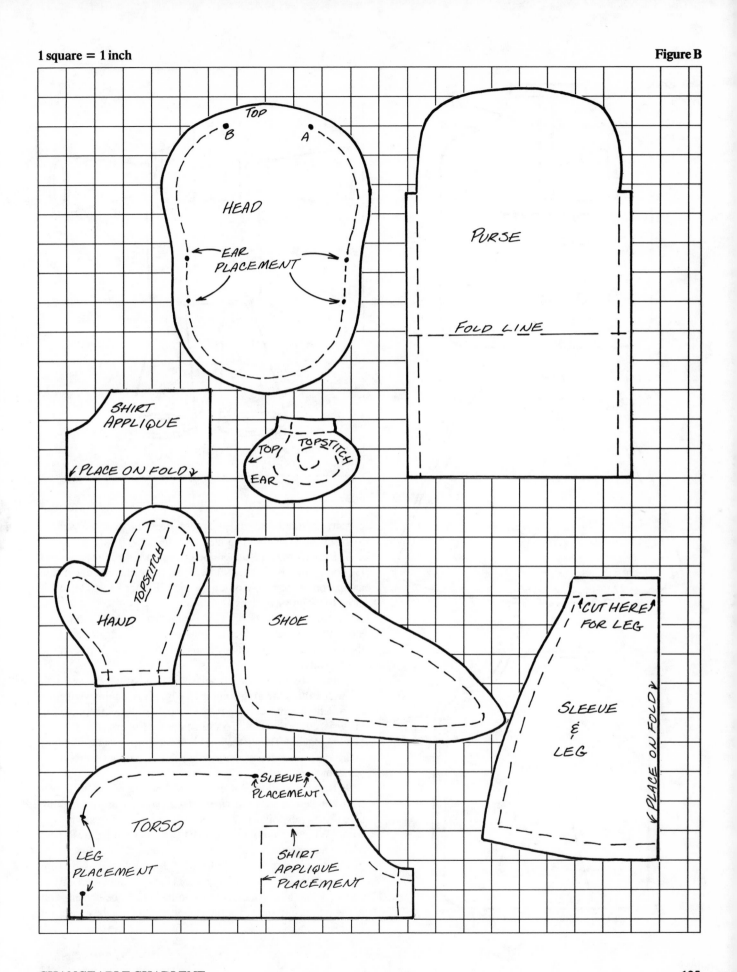

TOP

B   A

HEAD

EAR
PLACEMENT

PURSE

FOLD LINE

SHIRT
APPLIQUE

↳ PLACE ON FOLD ↲

TOP   TOPSTITCH

EAR

HAND

TOPSTITCH

SHOE

↳ CUT HERE ↲
FOR LEG

SLEEVE
&
LEG

↳ PLACE ON FOLD ↲

TORSO

SLEEVE
PLACEMENT

LEG
PLACEMENT

SHIRT
APPLIQUE
PLACEMENT

Figure C

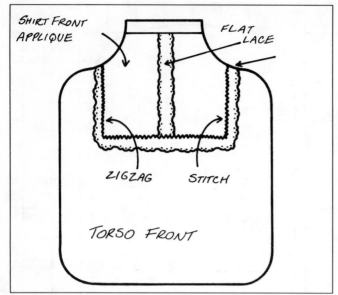

SHIRT FRONT APPLIQUE

FLAT LACE

ZIGZAG STITCH

TORSO FRONT

Figure D

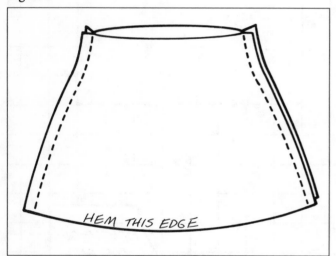

HEM THIS EDGE

Figure E

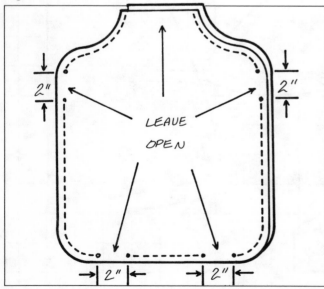

2" 2"

LEAVE OPEN

2" 2"

Figure F

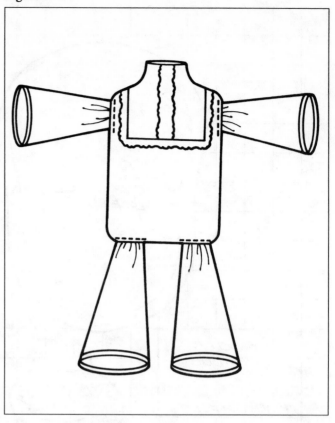

2-inch armhole and leg openings, as shown. Clip the curves and corners, turn right side out and press. Press the seam allowances to the inside along the openings. Stuff the torso firmly.

6. Baste across the unhemmed open end of each sleeve and leg and gather to 2 inches wide. Insert the gathered edge inside an appropriate armhole or leg opening (**Figure F**) and topstitch close to the pressed edges.

7. Place two Shoes right sides together and stitch the seam along the contoured edge, leaving the straight edge open. Clip the curves and turn right side out. Make a second shoe in the same manner.

8. Place two Hands right sides together. Stitch the seam all the way around the long contoured edge, leaving the wrist edge open. Clip the curves, turn right side out, stuff lightly and baste the wrist edges together. To soft-sculpt the fingers, topstitch (by hand or machine) along the lines indicated on the scale drawing, using flesh-tone heavy-duty thread. Make another hand in the same manner.

9. Baste around the lower edge of one sleeve, about 1 inch from the hem. Insert the wrist edge of a hand inside, making sure the thumb points upward, and gather the sleeve around the wrist. Whipstitch around the wrist to secure the hand. Repeat to attach the second hand.

10. Repeat step 9 to attach a shoe to each leg, making sure the toes point in the same direction as the appliqued torso front. Cut an 18-inch length of satin ribbon and tack the center point to the top of one shoe. Tie the ribbon into a large bow. Repeat for the second shoe.

GREAT FABRIC DOLL BOOK

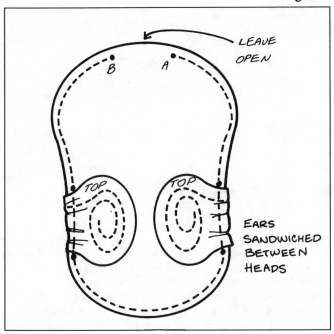

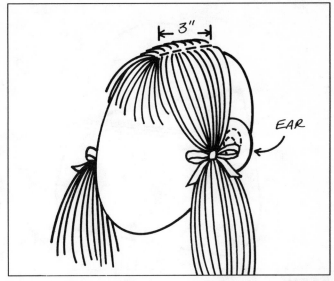

Figure I

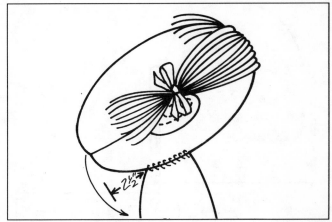

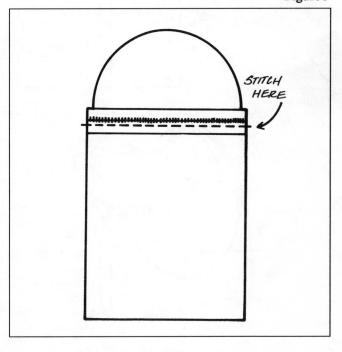

Making the Head

1. Place two Ears right sides together and stitch around the contoured edge, leaving the short straight edge open. Clip the curves and turn right side out but do not stuff. To soft-sculpt the ear, use flesh-tone heavy-duty thread and topstitch (by hand or machine) through both layers, following the spiral stitching line provided on the scale drawing. Repeat this step to assemble and soft-sculpt a second ear.

2. Baste the ears to one Head (**Figure G**), easing the edge of each ear to fit the placement marks on the scale drawing. Be sure the top of the ear points toward the top of the Head. Place the remaining Head right side down on top and stitch the seam, beginning at point **A** and ending at point **B**, as shown. Leave the seam open between **A** and **B**. Clip the curves, turn right side out and press the seam allowances to the inside along the opening. Stuff firmly and blindstitch the opening edges.

3. To make Charlene's hair, cut about one hundred 24-inch strands of yarn. Spread the strands across her head and back-stitch along the center part (**Figure H**). To create the bangs, pull about twenty strands to the front and trim them. To form the ponytails, tie together the remaining strands at ear level on each side, using a spare length of yarn. Tie a 12-inch length of satin ribbon into a bow and secure just in front of each ear.

4. Place the head over the open neck edge of the body, as shown in **Figure I**. The neck should be about 2½ inches behind the chin and the chin should point in the same direction as the front torso. Bend the head downward so the chin rests on the shirt. (You will have to tuck the neck edge under a bit at the front to get this right.) Whipstitch around the neck several times to secure the head. You may wish to tack the underside of the chin to the shirt just below the neck, to keep Charlene's head from wobbling.

5. All of Charlene's facial features are interchangeable, except her nose. To make the nose, baste around the perimeter of

CHANGEABLE CHARLENE

Figure K

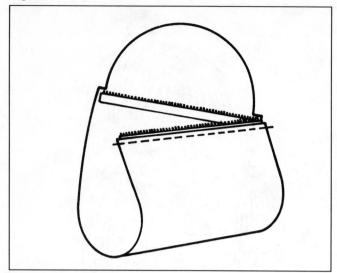

Figure L

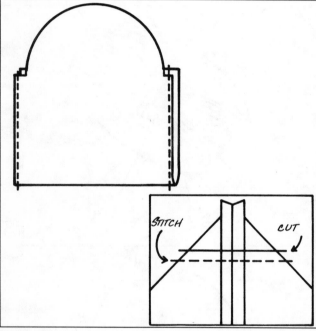

Figure M

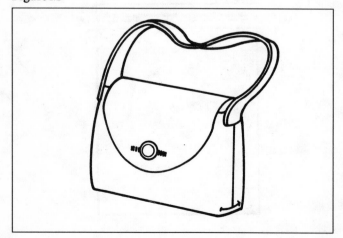

Figure N

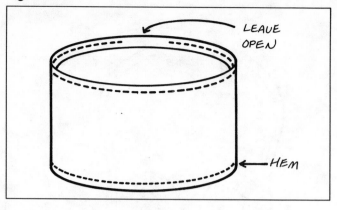

the 2-inch-diameter Nose. Place a small wad of fiberfill in the center and gather the fabric around it. Place the nose on her face (gathered edge down) and blindstitch to secure it.

6. Use the full-size patterns provided and cut the facial features from felt. We cut the Eyes from white, the Mouths from red and pink, the Irises from blue and the Eyebrows from black. You can create as many different facial features as you like; just let your imagination be your guide! Assemble matching pairs of Eye/Iris combinations, using glue to adhere the felt layers.

7. Cut small squares or circles of nylon fastener strip. Separate the halves and glue one half of each to the face at the placement markings indicated for the facial features (mouth, eyes and eyebrows). Glue the matching half of each fastener strip to the back of a facial feature. Be sure to use the proper halves on each piece or they will not stick to the face. Cut additional fastener squares or spots and glue the proper half of each to the back of an extra facial feature.

8. Stick a set of facial features on Charlene's face. After you make the purse, tuck the extras into it for safe keeping.

The Purse and Skirt

1. Place the closed zipper face down across the Purse just beneath the flap (**Figure J**). Stitch just below the zipper teeth and open the zipper.

2. Fold the lower end upward and pin the raw edge to the opposite side of the zipper (**Figure K**). Stitch, pulling the rest of the fabric out of the way, as shown. Turn wrong side out.

3. Stitch the side seams (**Figure L**) and press open. Square the lower corners, as shown in the inset. Clip the corners and turn right side out.

4. Glue or stitch the Purse Strap in place (**Figure M**). Work a buttonhole in the flap and stitch the button to the purse.

5. Fold the Skirt in half widthwise, placing right sides together. Stitch the side seam and press open.

6. Hem the lower edge of the skirt (**Figure N**). To make the waistline casing, turn under and stitch a double hem, leaving an opening to insert the elastic. Thread elastic through the casing, stitch together the ends and pull them back into the casing. Whipstitch the opening.

7. Dress Charlene in her skirt. Place her additional facial features in her purse. Put her purse over her arm and she's all ready to go to town.